Marx with Spinoza

Spinoza Studies
Series editor: Filippo Del Lucchese, Alma Mater Studiorum – Università di Bologna

Seminal works devoted to Spinoza that challenge mainstream scholarship
This series aims to broaden the understanding of Spinoza in the Anglophone world by making some of the most important work by continental scholars available in English translation for the first time. Some of Spinoza's most important themes – that right is coextensive with power, that every political order is based on the power of the multitude, the critique of superstition and the rejection of the idea of providence – are explored by these philosophers in detail and in ways that will open up new possibilities for reading and interpreting Spinoza.

Editorial Advisory board
Saverio Ansaldi, Etienne Balibar, Chiara Bottici, Laurent Bove, Mariana de Gainza, Moira Gatens, Thomas Hippler, Susan James, Chantal Jaquet, Mogens Laerke, Beth Lord, Pierre Macherey, Nicola Marcucci, Alexandre Matheron (1926–2020), Dave Mesing, Warren Montag, Pierre-François Moreau, Vittorio Morfino, Antonio Negri, Susan Ruddick, Martin Saar, Pascal Sévérac, Hasana Sharp, Diego Tatián, Francesco Toto, Dimitris Vardoulakis, Lorenzo Vinciguerra, Stefano Visentin, Manfred Walther, Caroline Williams.

Books available
Affects, Actions and Passions in Spinoza: The Unity of Body and Mind, Chantal Jaquet, translated by Tatiana Reznichenko
The Spinoza-Machiavelli Encounter: Time and Occasion, Vittorio Morfino, translated by Dave Mesing
Politics, Ontology and Knowledge in Spinoza, Alexandre Matheron, translated and edited by Filippo Del Lucchese, David Maruzzella and Gil Morejón
Spinoza, the Epicurean: Authority and Utility in Materialism, Dimitris Vardoulakis
Experience and Eternity in Spinoza, Pierre-François Moreau, edited and translated by Robert Boncardo
Spinoza and the Politics of Freedom, Dan Taylor
Spinoza's Political Philosophy: The Factory of Imperium, Riccardo Caporali, translated by Fabio Gironi
Spinoza's Paradoxical Conservatism, François Zourabichvili, translated by Gil Morejón
Marx with Spinoza: Production, Alienation, History, Franck Fischbach, translated by Jason Read

Forthcoming
Affirmation and Resistance in Spinoza: Strategy of the Conatus, Laurent Bove, translated and edited by Émilie Filion-Donato and Hasana Sharp
Spinoza and Contemporary Biology: Lectures on the Philosophy of Biology and Cognitivism, Henri Atlan, translated by Inja Stracenski
Spinoza's Critique of Hobbes: Law, Power and Freedom, Christian Lazzeri, translated by Nils F. Schott
Spinoza and the Sign: The Logic of Imagination, Lorenzo Vinciguerra, translated by Alexander Reynolds

Visit our website at www.edinburghuniversitypress.com/series/SPIN

Marx with Spinoza
Production, Alienation, History

Franck Fischbach

Translated by Jason Read

EDINBURGH
University Press

Edinburgh University Press is one of the leading university presses in the UK. We publish academic books and journals in our selected subject areas across the humanities and social sciences, combining cutting-edge scholarship with high editorial and production values to produce academic works of lasting importance. For more information visit our website: edinburghuniversitypress.com

La production des hommes. Marx avec Spinoza
Deuxième edition revue et corrigée
© Librairie Philosophique J. Vrin, 2014
www.vrin.fr
English translation © Jason Read, 2023, 2024

Edinburgh University Press Ltd
13 Infirmary Street, Edinburgh, EH1 1LT

First published in hardback by Edinburgh University Press 2023

Typeset in 10.5/13pt Goudy Old Style
by Cheshire Typesetting Ltd, Cuddington, Cheshire, and

A CIP record for this book is available from the British Library

ISBN 978 1 3995 0766 0 (hardback)
ISBN 978 1 3995 0767 7 (paperback)
ISBN 978 1 3995 0768 4 (webready PDF)
ISBN 978 1 3995 0769 1 (epub)

The right of Franck Fischbach to be identified as the author of this work has been asserted in accordance with the Copyright, Designs and Patents Act 1988, and the Copyright and Related Rights Regulations 2003 (SI No. 2498).

Published with the support of the University of Edinburgh Scholarly Publishing Initiatives Fund.

Contents

Reference Conventions	vi
Preface to the Second Edition	vii
Introduction: Spinoza, Marx and the Politics of Liberation	1
1. Marxism and Spinozism	13
2. *Pars Naturae*	22
3. Enduring Social Relations	27
4. The Identity of Nature and History	36
5. With Respect to Contradiction	60
6. The Secondary Nature of the Consciousness of Self	71
7. Subjectivity and Alienation (or the Impotence of the Subject)	79
8. The Factory of Subjectivity	92
9. Pure and Impure Activity	101
Conclusion: Metaphysics and Production	110
Appendix: The Question of Alienation: Frédéric Lordon, Marx and Spinoza	137
Bibliography	144
Index	149

Reference Conventions

All quotations from Spinoza's works in English are taken from Curley's two-volume *Collected Works of Spinoza* (CWS). For each citation, I provide a an internal reference to Spinoza's text using the conventions below, as well as a reference to the *CWS* volume and page number.

      Ethics   Ethics (Ethica Ordine Geomoetrico demostrata et in quinque Partes distincta). Roman numerals refer to Part number; Arabic numerals refer to Proposition number; further specifications follow the conventions below.

          TP   *Political Treatise* (*Tractatus Politicus*). Roman numerals refer to chapter number; Arabic numerals refer to paragraph number.

Alt. Dem	Alternative Demonstration
App.	Appendix
Ax.	Axiom
Cor.	Corollary
DA#	Definition of the Affects
Def.	Definition
Dem.	Demonstration
Exp.	Explanation
GDA	General Definition of the Affects
Lem.	Lemma
Post.	Postulate
Praef.	Preface
Prol.	Prolegomenon
Schol.	Scholium

Preface to the Second Edition

With the hindsight that is available to me today, at the moment of returning to a book which initially appeared in 2005, I can see that *Marx with Spinoza: Production, Alienation, History* (*La production des hommes*) began for me a path towards social criticism that found its complete realisation two books later, with *La privation de monde* (Vrin, 2011). This critical path was, in a sense, initially a negative path: it consisted in establishing a relation between the subjectivity of modernity, that is to the say the concept of the subject that has been elaborated by modern philosophy, and a negative and critical state, that is to say the general state of the crisis (certainly social and political, but without doubt also moral) that defines contemporary experience and that I conceive under the phrase 'loss of the world' or 'the privation of the world'. The subject separated from the world, thought as separate from or to the side of the world, and thereby separated from the objective conditions that make possible its accomplishment and its realisation, this subject which appears to have been conceived by philosophy as something which is *a priori*, has been socially instituted by a certain number of apparatuses characteristic of capitalist society. That is such that social formations of this type make the mass production of subjects deprived of the world, deprived of the access to objective conditions of true affirmation of themselves, the condition of their functioning and reproduction. I tried to confirm this hypothesis and to examine at least certain aspects of these apparatuses in the book that appeared between the two just mentioned, *Sans objet* (Vrin, 2009, republished in 2012).

The principal philosophical figures I have referred in these books have been Spinoza, Marx and Heidegger: three thinkers who have explicitly refused the idea that one can arrive at a true understanding of human existence by beginning with a subject separated from the rest of the world, thinking of it 'as a kingdom within a kingdom', or a subject which is only a subject in being without an object and separated from objectivity in all of its forms (natural, historical, and social). Additionally, these three thinkers are the critics par excellence of a subject without a world, of a subject which can only be thought and think of itself as a subject existing separately from the world as a reality from which it must be separated, in short, as an exception to the world. Spinoza, Marx and Heidegger have thus appeared to be the major representatives of a tradition critical towards 'the philosophers who isolate the individual, the subject';[1] though, of course, this critical tradition has other eminent representatives, including Dewey, who I have just cited. One finds expressed in these thinkers the thesis according to which it is not possible to arrive at a correct understanding of human existence if one does not start with its belonging to the objective world, its inscription within the objective totality, and, still more specifically, with the objective world that is society, that is to say the ensemble of connections within which human beings do not exist separately from each other any more than they exist separately from the world. Being in the world is always at the same time being one with others in relations of interaction: Spinoza speaks of the modes of human beings that originally and necessarily affect each other, Marx of *Verkehr* (*Commercium*) or 'the ensemble of social relations', Heidegger of *Mitsein* (being with), and Dewey of interaction.

Another characterisation of this tradition of thought is its approach to human beings, not just as they belong to the world – as inscribed and inserted in it, as '*partes naturae*', to use Spinoza's term later borrowed by Marx – but moreover as being part of the world through a certain activity. Human beings are approached not as subjects outside the world, but as beings inscribing themselves in it through the very activity they deploy. This activity is called is 'production' by Spinoza and 'labour' by Marx (and Heidegger). It is worth noting that this activity is inseparable from the dimension of relations, commerce and interaction already mentioned: there is reciprocal affection and connection only insofar as there is a deployment of activity which produces affects while also being affected. Everything in question follows from determining the proper nature of this activity: should it be called production or work? I return to this essential question in what follows.

Beginning from here one can also begin to envision that human beings are not simply found in their condition in the world but are also, within this condition, capable of utilising their activity to make of the world something more than how they simply find it: to make it a more habitable, human

---

[1] Dewey, *Art as Experience*, p. 373.

world, or, in other words, a social world. It is this perspective – that of the relations of individuals and the world between them, rather than an isolated subject – that leads me to consider my work as belonging in the domain and the tradition of social philosophy. Ever since the publication of *La production des hommes*, I have progressively engaged in work at a level that could be considered more constructive and less critical: human existence is, I have argued, characterised by the forms of activity that humans deploy more than by some substantial human essence. The question that then arises is this: what exactly is this activity that humans deploy, not just in terms of the world but also in terms of the social world? I respond that it is work, and that as such one cannot speak of social philosophy without at the same time focusing on the centrality of work. The negative and alienating effects of capitalist apparatuses are focused on work – beginning with the apparatus of the salary, which consists in separating working subjects from the objective conditions of their labour – but this does not restrict work, on the contrary, it explains that work is at the same time the basis for achievement and accomplishment: the activity of insertion in the world that makes opposition to the mechanisms of separation from the world possible for the very ones who are themselves victims of this separation. At the same time it also makes possible acts of coordination and cooperation that enable them to form social relations opposed to the processes of separation, individualisation and competition put to work by capital.

If one returns to Louis de Bonald's distinction between 'exterior man' and 'interior man', made in the course with his polemic with Maine de Biran, it is clear that the point of view of social philosophy as it is currently practised is that of the 'human exterior', in that it is always closer to a sociology than to a psychology. This implies two things: on the one hand a critique of the point of view of 'interior man' (the critique which has a privileged place in the work of Spinoza, Marx and Heidegger), according to which the reduction of humanity to an interiority is also a reduction to impotence; on the other hand, a valorisation of that activity by which human beings manifest precisely as exterior beings, as existing through the outside and therefore as being in the world – which is to say, labour. On this last point, one might object that of the three thinkers I have made reference to here, only Marx is a thinker of labour; one could say that there is in Spinoza a thought of production but not labour, while in Heidegger there is a critique of production (of an entire metaphysics of production) which is such that it can be extended into a critique of labour.

This leads directly to the usage I have made in the present work of the concepts of production and work. I now think that the limitation of my argument in *La production des hommes* was to have admitted without examining sufficiently that labour can be included not only as a figure of production, but moreover as a figure of the reduction of production, and therefore to have considered without further examination that capitalist modernity has been the theatre of a 'becoming labour of production', and that such a becoming amounts to a limitation, a weakening, of what production is and can do. At the end of the book I attempt to liberate production from Heidegger's criticism. But I now think that I got it backwards: saving labour from production is not a matter of leaving it to be dissolved in and by production. The point is that labour is positively and uniquely a human modality of production; one can therefore certainly continue, in the manner of Spinoza, to insert human production at the heart of natural production, with the qualification that human production takes the specific form of labour.

If it can be said that capitalist modernity is a theatre, it is not one of a reduction of production to labour, but of a reduction of human labour to an activity that is only production, or, to put in in terms of the tradition, to an activity that is only poietic. The entire effort has been to demonstrate (as is implicit in the *Economic and Philosophical Manuscripts of 1844* and becomes explicit from *The German Ideology* and the *Theses on Feuerbach*) that human labour cannot be reduced to poiesis, but must be recognized as the unity of poiesis and praxis. The activity of human beings in producing useful things is at the same time the activity of the formation and transformation of themselves. It is thus because the human activity of production that is labour is always a social activity that it that is socially divided, which places human beings at the same time in a condition of mutual dependence and reciprocal interaction. In other words, to put it in Spinoza's terms, if human beings are always mutually affected, it is the social division of labour that renders them mutually dependent upon each other. At the same time, it is this mutual dependence that human beings find themselves in, given the conditions and division of labour, that opens the horizon of a possible transformation of these relations that situate them from the outset; the horizon of a transformation from a division that is endured to a rationally, consciously, willed and organised division, and therefore also the practical (praxis) horizon of the formation of human beings in their labour and association. Capitalism strives to block this horizon of transformation which expands beyond its limited foundation, and one of the means it employs is precisely the reduction of work to a simple poiesis: the restriction of work to a purely productive activity that eliminates any practical element of training and self-transformation.

Introduction: Spinoza, Marx and the Politics of Liberation

What if, to conclude, we floated the idea that not only Spinoza, but Marx himself, Marx, the liberated ontologist, was a Marrano? A sort of clandestine immigrant, a Hispano-Portuguese disguised as a German Jew who, we will assume, pretended to have converted to Protestantism, and even to be a shade anti-Semitic? Now that would really be something.

Jacques Derrida, 'Marx & Sons'

The examination of the relation of Marx with Spinoza has often been driven – most notably with respect to Althusser and the Althusserian tradition – by the project of 'giving Marxism the metaphysics that it needs', according to an expression used by Pierre Macherey specifically with respect to Althusser. The intention was laudable, but, times having changed, our project can no longer be exactly that. We begin from the idea that the *philosophy* specific to Marx, or the specifically *Marxist philosophy*, is still largely unknown, that Marx as a *philosopher* is still largely and for the most part unknown. For a long time this was due to factors largely external to the thought of Marx: initially, the urgency of militant practice; later, the theme of the rupture with philosophy expressed by the eleventh Thesis on Feuerbach and in *The German Ideology*, which meant that any reading of Marx that was resolutely philosophical was suspected of being ideological. Then, at the margins of orthodoxy, several authors – and not insignificant ones – both at the heart of the history of Marxism[1] and

---

[1] We could mention, among others, the young Gentile (*The Philosophy of Marx*, 1899), Lukács (*History and Class Consciousness*, 1923), Bloch (*The Spirit of Utopia*, 1918), Korsch (*Marxism and Philosophy*, 1923), Gramsci (*Prison Notebooks*, 1929–35), Sartre (*Critique of Dialectical Reason*, 1960), Kosík (*Dialects of the Concrete*, 1962) and, of course, Althusser (*For Marx*, 1965).

outside of it,² maintained that while there is a critique of philosophy in Marx,³ this critique would still be a determinant practice of philosophy. The ignorance of 'Marx's philosophy', however, is equally due to factors internal to his work: the critical relation that Marx enters into with philosophy implies in effect that when it appears it does so in unfamiliar and novel ways, which are not those of a doctrine expressed as such – Marx, who never completed any of his grand works, always refused any dogmatic or systematic presentation of his thoughts – but are also not a matter of mere fragments. Neither systematic nor fragmentary, philosophy in Marx appears diluted, omnipresent but always mixed,⁴ and everywhere combined with elements of the discourses of history and political economy, but also the natural sciences and literature. It is not necessary to reconstruct or reconstitute the philosophy of Marx: that would suggest it is only present in a fragmentary and dispersed state, and that it is necessary to reassemble and unify it, leading to a dogmatic and systemic presentation that is perfectly alien to the Marxist practice of philosophy.

It would then be a matter of isolating – in the chemical sense of the term – the philosophy of Marx from the non-philosophical elements with which it is amalgamated, on the express condition of returning them to the 'compound', if only in order to see what it becomes, and the effects of the philosophical 'elements' when they come into contact with elements of another nature. The presupposition here, then, is quite different: it is no longer that of a dispersed philosophy of Marx waiting to be reassembled; it is that Marx's thought is in its entirety (one could say *from beginning to end*) infused, traversed, saturated with philosophy, including and perhaps especially when it appropriates objects and immerses itself in discourses that are not immediately philosophical. It is a matter then of revealing – in the photographic and chemical sense of the word – the philosophy of Marx. It is necessary to have a revealer. For reasons to be explained in what follows, we turn to Spinoza for this role as developer of Marx's philosophy, in a process

---

² One could think of Merleau-Ponty (*The Adventures of the Dialectic*, 1955), Henry (*Marx I and II*, 1976), Paul Ricoeur (*Ideology and Utopia*, 1986), and most recently, Derrida (*Specters of Marx*, 1993).

³ After the title of a work by Isabelle Garo, *Marx, Une Critique de la philosophie*, Paris: Le Seuil, 2000.

⁴ Which, by the way, means that there is no sense in sorting out the texts of Marx that would be considered philosophical and those that would be considered not – such as those Michel Henry calls the 'historico-political texts', within which figures, according to him, the *Communist Manifesto* (Henry, *Marx: A Philosophy of Human Reality*, 2). It is regrettable that such a division between philosophy and non-philosophy presides over the partial division of the works of Marx published by Pléiade.

which, it should be understood, does not begin with claiming that Marx is basically Spinoza or that Marx was a Spinozist. The book you are reading is not a work on Marx and Spinoza, treating them as two authors of two 'doctrines'; there is no such equilibrium. It acts first of all as a book on Marx, but of Marx read in the light of Spinoza, insofar as, in that light, the thought of Marx can be seen to be clearly and properly philosophical.

What result can we expect from such a process? To begin with, in advance, there is the simple idea that we find in Merleau-Ponty (but which could equally be found elsewhere) that 'the history that produces capitalism symbolizes the emergence of subjectivity'.[5] An equally simple question would be to ask whether this emergence is to the credit or the discredit of capitalism. For Merleau-Ponty it is clear that it is to its credit, and moreover that Marx himself credits capitalism with the emergence of a society conceived as the subject of its production of itself in which people conceive of themselves as subjects. Discussing Lukács in the same text, Merleau-Ponty recognises that he had the merit of elaborating 'a Marxism which incorporates subjectivity into history without making it an epiphenomenon'.[6] As for us, we come to the idea here that, if it is true that Marx makes the formation of subjectivity a phenomenon inseparable from the history of capitalism – and therefore something other than an 'epiphenomenon' (on this point Merleau-Ponty is right) – it can be seen to be exactly the opposite with respect to the emancipatory process. The history of capitalism, from its formation up to its overcoming, is not that of an increase of the power of subjectivity as the condition of all liberation – the contradiction unique to capitalism being to have formed at its centre the condition of its overcoming. If Marx had only said that, it would be a disarming simplicity, a childish dialectic that would not merit even an hour's attention: capitalism has produced subjectivity, but it does not produce it without at the same time oppressing and repressing it; hence what is to be done is to free it. In this way, from the retrospective point of view of an emancipated subjectivity, capitalism appears after such a break as a mode of production which has made a decisive contribution – albeit negatively and in some sense despite itself – in the liberation of humanity as a subject in and of itself. Depicted in such a way this simplistic version is not without its promoters (more within Marxism than among its adversaries), just because it is simple; but nothing could be more false than to seek in Marx yet another well-meaning description of the emergence of the modern subject as a history of progressive liberation.

---

[5] Merleau-Ponty, *Adventures of the Dialectic*, 38.
[6] Ibid., 41.

This is why the contemporary exhaustion of metanarratives of emancipation does not fundamentally concern Marx, so that we cannot infer from the exhaustion of the former the death of the latter.[7] It is a different history that Marx relates to us: what he was concerned with was uncovering the links that inseparably connect the birth of modern subjectivity to economic, political and ideological processes that have reduced the majority of people to a total lack of power. It was his task to show that the 'pure subjectivity' celebrated by theological, political, philosophical, moral, juridical and nowadays psychological and media discourses is in reality nothing other than the absolute naked exposure of human beings to powers of domination, constraint and subjection without precedence in history. The problem for Marx was not to examine the possibilities of the liberation of a subjectivity formed in capitalism and oppressed by it, but to comprehend and expose the social, economic and political processes that reduce humanity to a complete individual and collective impotence. In forming subjectivity capitalism has not produced the basis of its proper negation; on the contrary, it has engendered and produced an element absolutely indispensable to its own perpetuation.

In brief, our analysis has brought us to conclusions opposed to Merleau-Ponty's, notably when he writes that 'historical materialism . . . states a kinship between the person and the exterior, between the subject and the object, which is at the bottom of the alienation of the subject in the object and, if the movement is reversed, will be the basis for the reintegration of the world with man'.[8] If this is alienation for Marx then one is at pains to demonstrate in what way it differs from Hegel. Merleau-Ponty adds: 'Marx's innovation is that he takes this fact as fundamental, whereas, for Hegel, alienation is still an operation of the spirit on itself and thus is already overcome when it manifests itself.'[9] Alienation is thus not radical enough when it comes to Hegel precisely because it is already included within the activity of spirit. In Hegel, everything would thus play out in advance: if spirit is capable of going outside of itself, it is also always capable of being recovered and re-established, of returning to itself from itself having been posed by itself as something other than itself. The novelty of Marx consists, if one follows Merleau-Ponty, in refusing this facility, in not immediately reducing the loss of the subject in the object to an act of the subject itself, and instead

---

[7] This is what Derrida saw and wrote about in 1993, interpreting the ambient discourse of the end of emancipatory narratives and the death of Marx as a 'dominating discourse [which] often has the manic, jubilatory, and incantatory form that Freud assigned to the so-called triumphant phase of mourning work' (Derrida, *Specters of Marx*, 64).

[8] Merleau-Ponty, *Adventures of the Dialectic*, 33.

[9] Ibid.

starting from this loss as a fact, as the originary *Faktum*. Alienation would thus be a different and more serious affair, and would cease to be a sort of play of the subject with itself.

This understanding of the 'novelty' of Marx is not sufficient in our eyes, notably because it makes it impossible for us to comprehend the difference between Marx and Feuerbach, a difference that Marx never wanted to stop marking. One could also ask if such a view of alienation as a 'primitive fact' is compatible with a philosophy which, moreover, cannot comprehend alienation as anything other than the result of a historical process and not an ahistorical fact. This is why we interpret Marx's concept of alienation not as another version of the loss of the subject in the object, but as a radically new thought of the loss of objects that are essential and vital for an existence that is itself essentially objective and vital.[10] Alienation would not be a primitive fact, but the result of a process that we describe, following Étienne Balibar,[11] as the becoming-labour of production.

On the relation between 'the person and the exterior', Merleau-Ponty is right; but he does not see how this relation is radicalised by Marx: it is not necessary to restrict the 'person' to the status of the subject. In other words, the relation of humanity with the world is for Marx the fact that the human being is immediately[12] a being of the world, or, as he writes in the *Economic*

---

[10] According to a model that is omnipresent in Hegel, since it is he who makes it possible to express the truth of the concept of spirit: 'However, spirit has shown itself to us to be neither the mere withdrawal of self-consciousness into its pure inwardness, nor the mere immersion of self-consciousness into substance and the non-being of its difference. Rather, it has shown itself to be this movement of the self which relinquishes itself of itself and immerses itself in its substance, and which likewise as subject, has both taken the inward turn into itself from out of that substance and has made its substance into an object and a content' (Hegel, *The Phenomenology of Spirit*, 464). If for Feuerbach the subject is no longer spirit but the essence of humanity, nevertheless the model of the exteriorisation of the subject in the object and the return of the self from the object remains the model through which it is possible to think of alienation and its overcoming: 'religion is the first, but indirect, self-consciousness of man ... man transposes his essential being outside of himself before he finds it within himself. His own being becomes the object of his thought first as another being' (Feuerbach, *The Fiery Brook*, 110).

[11] Balibar, *Masses, Classes, and Ideas*, 93.

[12] 'Man is directly a *natural being*' Marx writes in 1844 (*Early Writings*, 389), while showing that the most important part of this proposition is what is not underlined. No one has seen better than Granel the importance of this thought (which is both anti-Hegelian and Spinozist) of immediacy which permits Marx to posit that human beings and nature are not simply in 'a relation' the one with the other. See Granel, 'L'ontologie marxiste de 1844 et la question de la 'coupure', 185–6.

and *Philosophical Manuscripts of 1844*, an 'objective being', conceived according to an expression of Spinoza's reprised by Marx as part of nature (*pars naturae, Teil de Natur*). This leads Marx to totally rethink the concept of alienation: it is not a loss of the subject in the object, but rather consists, for objective beings such as humans, in a loss of their 'essential objects'; that is to say, the loss of their proper objectivity ('because a being which has no object outside of itself does not have objective being' and 'a non-objective being is a non-being'[13]). It is precisely this loss of objectivity that constitutes essentially the becoming subject of humanity,[14] in other words, the formation of the modern subject: subjectivity befalls precisely the being from whom the objective dimension of its existence has been withdrawn, from whom all of its vital and essential objects (those on which it depends in order to persevere in its being) have been subtracted. Alienation is not therefore the loss of the subject in the object; it is 'the loss of object'[15] for a being that is itself objective. But the loss of its objects and of the objectivity of its proper being is also the loss of any possible inscription of its activity in objectivity; it is the loss of all possible mastery of objectivity, among other effects. In short, becoming subject is essentially a reduction to impotence. The becoming subject or the subjectivation of human beings is thus inseparable, according to Marx, from that which is absolutely indispensable for capitalism: the existence of a mass of 'naked workers' – that is to say, pure subjects as possessors of a perfectly abstract capacity to work; individual agents of a purely subjective power of labour who are constrained to sell its use to another to the same extent that they are totally dispossessed of the objective conditions (the means and tools of production, matter to work on) required to put to actual work their capacity to work.

[13] Marx, *Early Writings*, 390.
[14] One could certainly object that if alienation is the loss of objectivity by an objective being, then it is not in that sense uniquely human, since all natural beings are objective and all could lose their proper objectivity. But human beings are, for Marx, more objective beings than others (a difference of degree not of nature). First, because they can form more relations of objectivity, due to their specific corporal conformation; second, because they are not content simply to find objects that meet their needs, but produce them; third, because they not only produce the immediate objects of their need but also go beyond immediate need; fourth, because they are the only beings capable (by their knowledge) of entering into relation with all of nature; fifth, because in producing their essential objects human beings become objects for each other, becoming thus essential objects for each other and affirming their being in their relations with each other. This is also why only human beings are capable of totally losing their objectivity and living and conceiving of themselves as *subjects*.
[15] Marx, *Early Writings*, 386.

Under these conditions, the perspective of emancipation and liberation cannot consist, as Merleau-Ponty has it, in 'the reintegration of the world in humanity', but, to the contrary, only in the reintegration of humanity in the world: it is not a matter of reabsorbing the object in the subject, but of realising the subject in the object, of desubjectivising human beings and reobjectivating them in a world which is no longer a world *for* them, but the conditions of which are in them, as part of a vital and objective relation of dependence. Emancipation thus does not consist in integrating the world into humanity but in realising humanity in the world.

It is necessary on this point, as on others, to be attentive to the letter of Marx's text. Here, for example, in *The Holy Family*:

> if man takes all knowledge, sensation, etc., from the sensible world, and the experience at the heart of the world, what matters is how to organise the empirical world in such a way that man experiences it and becomes accustomed to what is truly human; let him experience his quality as a human being in the world . . . if human beings are made by experiences we must make experiences humanly.[16]

To human beings grasped as a subject outside of the world, confronted with an alien objectivity that they must reintegrate into themselves, Marx opposes the inverse process of the reinscription and reinsertion of humans in the world such that people are made in the world, can experience their 'human qualities', and get used to what is human. If there is for Marx a humanisation of the world, its precondition is the worlding of humanity. Only on this precondition can one understand that the humanisation of the world is not a human interiorisation of the world, a subjectivation of the object (that is to say as a purely speculative play of the subject with itself), but rather that this process of humanisation unfolds entirely in the immanence of a world understood as pure exteriority to itself, without interiority – and that this implies and imposes a practical and active transformation of the world as it is.[17]

---

[16] Marx and Engels, *The Holy Family*, 176 (Translator's note: translation modified following the French edition edited by Cogniot that Fischbach cites).

[17] It is worth noting that if there is a humanism in the texts of 1845 such as *The Holy Family*, it functions as a specific and paradoxical humanism: it lies at the foundation of an anti-humanism if by humanism one understands the ideal of a human essence independent of the world. Marx explains to the contrary that there only exist human beings *of* and *in* the world: he derives the non-humanist consequences of the sensualist humanism of Feuerbach (a sensualist humanism is by definition untenable and contradictory, since all humanism is an idealism – as Althusser has rightfully argued).

To put it briefly, as Spinoza did before him and as Heidegger would after him, Marx does not begin with the subject but with the world, with a situation of the world understood as an unlimited ensemble without beginning or end, that is to say as a non-totalisable totality of social-historical relations woven together with the natural and living existence of humans determined to produce the means for the permanent perpetuation of their existence in the world. When one begins from the world and not the subject, from the exterior and not the interior, from a plane of immanence rather than any position of exteriority, foundation, or transcendence, the task cannot be to bring the exterior back into the interior (interiorise the exterior), nor to return the world to the subject (subjectivise the object). Beginning from the exterior, from what Marx refers to as 'circumstances' – that is to say from the world insofar as it is an unlimited ensemble of relations necessarily engendered by encounters that are themselves contingent – one arrives at human beings as products of those circumstances, which is to say that human beings are always fundamentally beings that are affected, and therefore beings for which the relation with the world is primarily of the order of an encounter with events that happen in the world. Thus, starting from there, the task, as Marx says, is one of forming these circumstances humanely.

Which means what? Certainly not that one acts to transform the world in such a way that human subjectivity recognises itself and rediscovers itself, is able to see the world as a moment of its own auto-objectification, as indispensable to its return to itself. Considering that human beings, in their existence in *the* world, are not at all subjects exterior to the world, but are also products, themselves objective, of quotidian circumstances, of events and encounters, in the sense of what happens to them from and in the world, 'forming these circumstances humanely' cannot mean for Marx forming them in a manner such that they conform or are adequate to the essence of a humanity which is already posited. It cannot mean 'giving circumstances a human form', since that would entail a return to the supposition that the human form or essence can exist for and by itself independent of and prior to circumstances – which Marx denies.

To understand what is at stake here, it is necessary to proceed from the fact that in the world as it is, the majority of the circumstances that effect human beings – most of the events that happen to them, and the encounters they undergo – are not favourable or useful to them, that people are the products of circumstances, events and encounters that are neither generally nor immediately favourable or useful. From there, 'forming circumstances humanly' means firstly to produce and engender as many situations as possible and to select the maximum of encounters that are useful and favourable to human beings, in other words those that will aid and affirm their existence and their persevering in their being. The transformation of the world must first be grasped as a question of its reorganisation: a question of organising the world in such a way that events, circumstances and encounters favourable to human beings multiply in number and intensity to the point where they can find in the world a human way of living. Far from beginning with a predetermined essence of man that must be realised in the world by transforming the world, human beings, according to Marx, are only able to grasp what it is to be human on the condition of organising the world such that events favourable and useful to human beings are multiplied.

The concept of habitude, introduced here by Marx, is decisive: it is clearly a reference to Aristotle's concept of *hexis*, via Hegel's reprise of the same theme in his Introduction to the *Elements of the Philosophy of Right*, where, in defining the 'world of spirit' or the objective spirit of 'second nature',[18] Hegel indicates that the ethical world is that in which human beings actually form themselves as human through their integration into institutions (family, civil society, corporations and, finally, the institution that encompasses the former and founds them: the state), within which they experience the repetition of an always already objectified humanity.[19] On this basis, Marx writes that 'what has to be done is to arrange the empirical world in such a way that . . . man experiences and becomes accustomed to what is truly human in it'.[20] Far from knowing immediately what it is to be human – and then deriving a practical norm from the knowledge of this essence in order to orient the transformation of the world so as to make it conform with what it must be – it is on the contrary through their experience of the world that human beings are susceptible to progressively understanding what it means to be human. The difference with Hegel, however, is that for Marx this habitude does not entail a reference to the problem of the institution of a second nature irreducible to a first nature: closer to Aristotle than Hegel, Marx considers habitude to be the formation of a natural character which does not function as an essence valued as a norm that is itself superimposed and finally substitutes itself for nature. The formation of human character

---

[18] Hegel, *Elements of the Philosophy of Right*, 35.
[19] Taking habit as the element of ethics (Hegel, *Elements of the Philosophy of Right*, 195), by the repeated practice of a normativity inscribed and objectively deposed in institutions (familial, social, political), is for humans, according to Hegel, taking habit as that which is human, not abstractly (in conformity with an eternal essence of humanity), but concretely, that is to say in the heart of a human community historically instituted.
[20] Marx, *The Holy Family*, 176. Translation modified.

is not a function of a sense of humanity that is already present in the world and objectified in the institutions of 'second nature' that make up 'ethical life'; rather it is the function of a model of the human which human beings become immanently aware of through their experiences of what suits them by nature, in other words, of what is useful and favourable to them. Thus the problem for Marx is how to organise the world in such a way that one is able to multiply events and opportunities in which human beings experience what the Economic and Philosophical Manuscripts of 1844 calls their 'activation' (Betätigung), that is, a confirmation (Bestätigung) of themselves which is also a renewal of their being and an increase in their individual and collective capacity to act.[21]

It is then with subjectivity as it is with philosophy, if only because the latter has essentially been presented up to now as the thought of the former: one cannot realise it without negating it, or negate it without realising it. Reobjectifying humans, that is, negating their subjectivity as an otherworldly subjectivity, means negating that they are subjects exterior to the world that act on it insofar as it is an object; but at the same time it means adopting a point of view in which what philosophers call 'human subjectivity' appears as a reality that effectively and objectively exists in the world. What remains of what has been called subjectivity when one undertakes to make it worldly, objective and natural? What follows is that activity (Tätigkiet), more specifically vital productive activity, is to be understood not as the production of objects by subjects (that is, as productive labour,[22] which is not the same thing as productive activity), but as a production which is always at the same time auto-production, a production of the self by the self, and thus a confirmation and activation of the self. The activity by which human beings constitute themselves as objective beings, as things in the world, is thus at the same time a destructive activity which, in the same world, constitutes the reduction of human beings to the impotence of a bare and otherworldly subjectivity. Human beings are only able to affirm their effective power by destroying at the same time the real causes of their lack of power: this is why 'The coincidence of the changing of circumstances and of human activity or self-changing can be conceived and rationally understood only as *revolutionary practice*.'[23] If 'communism is the real movement that destroys

---

[21] Marx, Early Writings, 389.
[22] Or what Marx calls, in the texts of his maturity, the process of capitalist production insofar as it is the unity of the labour process and the valorisation process. See for example Marx, Economic Manuscripts of 1861–1863, 256.
[23] Marx, Early Writings, 422.

the present state of things',[24] it is because communism is the process of the negation and destruction of the actual circumstances that reduce human beings to impotence, that separate them from their power. This is not just a theoretical transformation, in which human beings shift from a conception of themselves as subjects to a conception of themselves as 'beings of nature', but a practical transformation effectively lived as an increase of power, as the individual and collective appropriation of a hitherto unknown power. Communism is therefore the real process, the ethical experience, by which people in changing life also change *their* life.

Returning human beings to the world: this was already Feuerbach's project, but for Marx it is not sufficient – all it can do is return to *Anschauung*, that is, a sensible intuition that is essentially contemplative and therefore passive. Overcoming this conception (which Spinoza calls imaginary) of human beings as subjects exterior to the world and for which there is an objective world can only be achieved through a massive transformation of their relation to their own humanity, that is to say through a practical transformation of their consciousness of self, and therefore through a self-production and self-engendering of new ways of being a self and a thing in the world. This is what makes philosophy, for Marx as well as Spinoza, a properly ethical transformation of the self, a radical modification, in theory and practice, of the self and the world. But can one transform one's way of being without at the same time revolutionising the world, that is to say without reorganising practically the space in which the self is proven and confirmed?

To the question that Foucault poses, 'How can the world, which is given as the object of knowledge on the basis of the mastery of *tekhne*, at the same time be the site where the "self" as ethical subject of truth appears and is experienced?',[25] and that he considered to be the fundamental problem of western philosophy, Marx, had he been able to respond, would say that the world, as the natural world, is not for beings that – as human beings – are themselves part of nature, as an external object to be known via *tekhne*, and that, as a historical world (but in truth it is always the same world that one acts in), it is not, in the actual state of things, a space where 'one' can test 'oneself' as an ethical subject of truth[26] – and that it can only become so at the price of its radical transformation. Moreover, from Marx's point of view, the two aspects of the question formulated by Foucault are indissociable: the

---

[24] Marx and Engels, *The German Ideology*, 57.
[25] Foucault, *The Hermeneutics of the Subject*, 487.
[26] Ibid.

world can only become the space of a real and positive experience of the self – an experience which is also an affirmation of the self – on condition of surmounting the conditions which make the world a simple object delivered over to *tekhne* or to subjects. These conditions have their existence primarily in the mode of production: it is in this element that they reduce the self to the impotence of the subject and the world to the objectivity of a manipulable object. It is these conditions that engender the separation between, one the one side, subjects as owners of a purely subjective labour power, and, on the other, the objective conditions that put this power to work (in as much as these conditions appear to be less the conditions of the labour process than the conditions of the valorisation of capital[27]). This separation makes it so that the subjective power of labour is defined as an impotent power, a power that can do nothing by itself because it is separated from the conditions of its proper objectivity. Conquering the objective conditions for an affirmative and powerful experience, for the joy of the self in the world, engendering the conditions for individual and collective self-affirmation – this, for both Spinoza and Marx, is what it means to change one's life.

---

[27] Marx, *Economic Manuscripts of 1861–1863*, 256.

1
Marxism and Spinozism

It is necessary to arrive at a certain form of unity, a space, between two diverse philosophers: the entire question is to know if this is possible without falling into the confusion that purely and simply identifies two philosophers with the fiction of a common truth.

Pierre Macherey, *Hegel or Spinoza*

Most know the role that Spinoza played in German philosophy at the turn of the nineteenth century in the famous 'pantheism controversy'[1] (which continued into the debate over atheism[2]). Most also know the importance that Hegel attributed to Spinoza's thought[3] ('Spinoza or no philosophy at all' stated the philosopher of Berlin). The presence of Spinoza throughout the philosophy of Schelling, from beginning to end, is also relatively well known.[4] However, it seems that far fewer know about the role played by the reference to Spinoza at the end of the remarkable sequence of German Idealism, and notably in the period following the death of Hegel in 1831.[5] There was a significant return of Spinoza, which was at the same time a

---

[1] See Sylvain Zac, *Spinoza en Allemagne. Mendelssohn, Lessing et Jacobi*; 'La renaissance de Spinoza dans la philosophie religieuse en Allemagne à l'époque de Goethe'; and 'Jacobi critique de Spinoza'.
[2] Estes and Bowman, eds., *Fichte and the Atheism Dispute (1798–1800)*.
[3] See the indispensable work by Pierre Macherey, *Hegel or Spinoza*.
[4] Jean-Marie Vaysse has dedicated a classic work of scholarship to the German reception of Spinoza from Lessing to the later Schelling, passing through Fichte, Hölderlin, the Romantic school and Hegel. See his *Totalité et subjectivité: Spinoza dans l'idéalisme allemand*.
[5] See the presentation (notably the first point entitled 'Spinoza or Feuerbach') by Jean Pierre Osier in his translation of *L'essence de christianisme* by Feuerbach (Paris: Maspero, 1968).

return to Spinoza, in the period opened up by Hegel's achievement of speculative idealism, and more precisely in the period of the decomposition of the Hegelian system, which began in earnest from 1838 with the divide between the 'old' and 'young' Hegelians, accentuated by the publication of Feuerbach's *The Essence of Christianity* in 1841 and by Marx's own works between 1843 and 1846. This is the moment when Spinoza becomes not only an explicit point of reference, but also an explicitly positive reference, most notably in the work of Heine and Moses Hess. After the publication in 1833 of Feuerbach's *History of Modern Philosophy from Bacon to Spinoza*, Hess published in 1937 his first book, the *Holy History of Mankind*, with no indication of the author's identity other than as 'a disciple of Spinoza'. As a thinker of the unity of all life, and of 'the one' as life, Spinoza is for Hess the thinker of the unity of natural life and spiritual life: his doctrine contained, in larval form, the reconciliation of Schelling's philosophy of Nature and Hegel's philosophy of Spirit prior to their development. It thus prepared the way for the philosophy of the future, which would reunite in action the activity of the self and the absolute and its activity outside the self.[6] 'The first truly speculative philosopher', writes Hess, 'is Spinoza: as with Christ, who he follows, who had begun the mediation of the ideal and the real, spirit and nature, with Spinoza this mediation arrives at his conclusion'.[7] It was still necessary that this mediation not only exist, but that it go outside of itself and become conscious of itself: it was this, in the eyes of Hess, that allowed Hegel and Schelling to achieve in ideality the unity of the ideal and the real that action will posit in reality.

It is in the context of this post-Hegelian return to Spinoza that we can situate the relation of Marx himself to Spinoza. If Marx, in contrast to Hess, never explicitly presents himself as 'a disciple of Spinoza', that does not mean that we should conclude, in following Marx's own work, that Spinoza was less important for him than certain of his contemporaries. It is nonetheless true that references to Spinoza have a greater importance in the history of Marxism than in the writings of Marx himself. It is easy to see that a non-negligible number of philosophers who have reclaimed Marx have also declared themselves to be Spinozists: the most well-known case is that of Althusser who, in *Reading Capital*, writes that 'Spinoza's philosophy introduced an unprecedented theoretical revolution in the history of philosophy . . . we can regard Spinoza as Marx's only direct ancestor from the philosoph-

---

[6] Hess, *Berlin, Paris, Londres, La triarchie Européen*, 63–4.
[7] Ibid., 90.

ical standpoint'.[8] Althusser adds that his own work is engaged on 'a path which was opened for us ... by two philosophers in history: Spinoza and Marx'; this path is one in which in the order of knowledge is aimed against both empiricism and idealism (of either the Cartesian, Kantian, or Hegelian variety) in which 'the *object* of knowledge or essence was in itself absolutely distinct and different from the *real object*'.[9]

But Althusser is not an isolated case, since the reference to Spinoza has been as equally important as the reference to Marx for Jean-Toussaint Desanti, Pierre Macherey,[10] Étienne Balibar,[11] Alexandre Matheron,[12] André Tosel,[13] Jacques Bidet and Antonio Negri.[14] If one goes further back in time one finds in the history of Marxism an abundance of other thinkers for whom the reference to Spinoza was also essential, including Karel Kosík and Ernst Bloch, but also Antonio Labriola and the Master of Lenin's thought, Georgi Plekhanov.[15] According to the latter, 'it was the Spinozism of Feuerbach that Marx and Engels adopted in breaking with idealism'.[16] Beyond this, it is possible to think that, for Marx at least, there is not first the rupture with idealism and then the adoption of a Spinozism through Feuerbach's naturalism. On the contrary, it is the adoption of a naturalism that has as its sources both Feuerbach and Spinoza that entails the rupture with idealism, and more particularly with Hegel. Beside this then, the attribution of Spinoza to Feuerbach by Plekhanov is made at the cost of a misunderstanding, which is not to say a misinterpretation. Plekhanov

[8] Althusser, 'The Object of Capital', in *Reading Capital*, 250.
[9] Althusser, 'From Capital to Marx's Philosophy', in *Reading Capital*, 40.
[10] Co-author of *Reading Capital*, Macherey has published a five-volume commentary on the entirety of the *Ethics*.
[11] Also a co-author of *Reading Capital*, Balibar is the author of *Spinoza and Politics* and 'Spinoza, the Anti-Orwell' in *Masses, Classes, and Ideas*.
[12] In an interview Matheron had the occasion to declare: 'At the start . . . I began studying Spinoza because I saw in him somebody who had the great merit, beyond the limits imposed on him by his class position, of being a precursor to Marx; and now, instead, I tend to see in Marx somebody who had the great merit of being one of the successors of Spinoza in certain domains.' ('Appendix 1: Interview with Laurent Bove and Pierre François Moreau', in *Politics, Ontology, and Knowledge in Spinoza*, 360.)
[13] Tosel is a specialist in Italian Marxism and the author of *Spinoza ou le crepuscule de la servitude* (Paris: Aubier, 1984) and a number of articles on Spinoza.
[14] Part of the grand tradition of Italian Marxism, Antonio Negri is also the author of *The Savage Anomaly*, a book that profoundly reinterprets Spinoza in order to separate his thought from the tradition of dialectical philosophy.
[15] Plekhanov, *The Fundamental Problems of Marxism*.
[16] On the use of Spinoza in Labriola and Plekhanov see André Tosel's study 'Des usages "Marxistes" de Spinoza: Leçon de method'.

in effect claims that, since Spinoza interprets 'natural phenomena as acts of God',[17] the consequence of this is that Spinozism maintains a theological dimension, even a form of divine transcendence. This is, according to Plekhanov, 'an important shortcoming in Spinoza's philosophy', and Feuerbach, in substituting *aut Deus au natura* for Spinoza's *Deus sive natura*, has restored Spinoza's heritage and stripped off what Plekhanov calls its 'theological pendant'. Thus, 'Feuerbach's "humanism" proved to be nothing else but Spinozism disencumbered of its theological pendant',[18] which exposed 'the true materialist content' of Spinoza's doctrine. It is thus this Spinozism that Marx claims as his heritage. One must recall, however, that Plekhanov's insistence on the Spinozism of Feuerbach as the predecessor of Marx occurs in a particular context: in Plekhanov's text published in 1908, it acts first against the neo-Kantianism principally represented by Bernstein, and works to affirm the existence of a veritable Marxist philosophy in contrast to the tendency to reduce Marx's thought to either a sociology or a Kantian ethics.[19] This is developed through the thesis according to which the philosophy of Marx rests on a Spinozist ontology, that is to say an atheological, immanent and materialist ontology. Marx would thus 'revitalize the [Spinozist] substance as historical materialist matter, [as] the metabolism of man with nature', renewing materialism in terms of its 'insufficient dialectical historical dimension'.[20] However, following Plekhanov means accepting two things that seem to us contestable: first the idea that Marx repeats the Hegelian understanding of Spinoza's substance as dead substance, immobile and fixed, so that it becomes necessary to infuse this substance with a principle of movement, of processes of development; second, that there remains in the Spinozist doctrine a theological dimension that it is necessary to free it from. On these two points it is possible to affirm firstly that Marx, contra Hegel, clearly perceived that, far from being fixed and static, the Spinozist substance is on the contrary infinitely productive and active. As Spinoza writes: 'God's power is nothing except God's active essence', and that 'it is as impossible for us to conceive that God does not act as it is to conceive that he does not exist'.[21] In other words, if Marx recovered something from Spinoza, it seems to us that it was exactly his conception of substance insofar as it is engaged in an ontology of production as an activity that is infinitely,

[17] Plekhanov, *The Fundamental Problems of Marxism*.
[18] Ibid.
[19] Ibid.
[20] Tosel, 'Des usages "Marxistes" de Spinoza: Leçon de méthode', 520.
[21] Spinoza, *Ethics* II, 3 Schol.; CWS I, 449.

naturally, necessarily and materially productive. Second, as we see it, Marx also perceived that Spinozism makes it possible to escape the sterile alternatives that trapped the young Hegelians: with Spinoza one is able to move beyond the oppositions of materialism and spiritualism, atheism and theism, objectivism and subjectivism, passivity and activity and thereby overcome the dualisms that Marx also intends to overcome.[22] Far from presenting a Spinozism that must be reformed to remove the embarrassment of its 'theological appendix' (especially if this appendix is nothing other than that of the first part of the *Ethics*), as Plekhanov insists, Marx understood that Spinoza's ontology of natural productive activity was from the beginning a fundamentally atheological ontology – one that is presented as an ongoing apparatus for the critique of the theological dimension of every ontology until now, including Hegel's. It is certainly Spinoza who made it possible for Marx to go beyond the position of abstract atheism at the heart of the *Introduction to Hegel's Philosophy of Right*; thus it is more the *Economic and Philosophical Manuscripts of 1844* that we consider to be the most profoundly Spinozist of Marx's texts, insofar as it marks out a distance between itself and an abstract atheism, which is criticised at the same time as 'crude' communism.[23]

Returning for a moment to Althusser – certainly one of the Marxist philosophers for whom the reference to Spinoza is most significant and most profound – the declaration of Spinozism in *Reading Capital* is returned to in 1975 in Althusser's 'Soutenance d'Amiens' (published in English as 'Is it Simple to Be a Marxist in Philosophy'.) Here Althusser declares that he had to 'refer back to Spinoza in order to understand why Marx had to refer back to Hegel'.[24] It is possible to read this as indicating that, at least in the Marxist tradition, comprehending Marx's relationship to Spinoza must pass through the intermediary of comprehending Hegel's relationship to Spinoza; perhaps this is why the great book on the relationship of Hegel to Spinoza is the work of a student of Althusser, also a Spinozist and a Marxist.[25] One might then be led to the conclusion that there is no direct relation of Marx to Spinoza, but only an indirect relation that passes through the intermediary of Hegel. Marx's Spinoza would then be essentially that of Hegel, in the sense that Marx retained the positive elements of Spinozism that Hegel

---

[22] These, in effect, are the oppositions enumerated by Marx in the *Economic and Philosophic Manuscripts of 1844*.
[23] Marx, *The Economic and Philosophic Manuscripts of 1844*.
[24] Althusser, 'Is It Simple to Be a Marxist in Philosophy', 206.
[25] Macherey, *Hegel or Spinoza*.

also retained. The eventual Spinozism of Marx would thus be the same Spinozism as Hegel's, and the proximity of Marx to Spinoza would be only a proximity to the Spinoza in Hegel. This is the hypothesis of Althusser when he writes: 'Marx was close to Hegel just in respect to all of the features that Hegel had openly borrowed from Spinoza.' More precisely: 'Marx was close to Hegel in his insistence on rejecting every philosophy of the Origin and of the Subject . . . in his critique of the cogito, of the sensualist-empiricist subject and of the transcendental subject', but also in 'his critique of the legal subject and of the social contract, in his critique of the moral subject, in short of every philosophical ideology of the Subject'.[26] If this is true then one can say if Marx is close to Hegel it is because he is close to the Spinozist in him.

The problem with this is that it returns us to that which is in Hegel but is not Hegel, and therefore to an abstraction from what is properly Hegel in Hegel, most notably from all those aspects of Hegel that are not the critique of the modern philosophy of the subject but, on the contrary, amount to its completion. Because even if it can be said that Hegel is a critic of the Cartesian cogito and of the transcendental subject of Kant, as well as a critic of the moral and juridical subject, his critique is not a pure and simple rejection of them, but makes them into internal moments of the development of a truer moment of subjectivity. For Hegel, they become finite, abstract, one-sided figures that must be integrated, as proper moments, into a true figure of subjectivity as the infinite and concrete subject of Spirit. We would then propose the hypothesis that, if the relation of Marx to Spinoza passes through Hegel, as Althusser argued, it is not in order to recover Hegel's Spinozism but on the contrary because Marx needed Spinoza in order to escape from Hegel, in the sense that Marx played Spinoza off against Hegel. Spinoza would then be the condition of possibility for a radical critique of that which is internal to Hegel, namely modern philosophy as an idealist metaphysics and a theology of subjectivity.

With the help of Spinoza, or by means of a detour through his work, it is possible to articulate three elements of Marx's thought that are also three elements of a philosophy common to Spinoza and Marx: 1) the thesis of the secondary nature of self-consciousness; 2) the thesis of the identity of nature and history; 3) the thesis of an ontology of productive activity. However, one cannot claim for a fact that Marx actually derived these elements from Spinoza. They are more of an index than anything else. As André Tosel has noted: 'The history of the role of Spinoza's thought in the

---

[26] Althusser, 'Is It Simple to Be a Marxist in Philosophy, 216.

formation of Marx's work remains to be written.'[27] We know for a fact that Marx had read Spinoza's *Tractatus Theologico-Politicus* as well as the correspondence, and had copied passages from them in 1841.[28] When it comes to the *Ethics*, Marx seems to have been familiar with it as a student, at least if one believes the indications given by the editors of the Marx-Engels Gesamtausgabe (MEGA).[29] However, as Gérard Benussan remarks in his article on 'Spinozism' in the *Dictionnaire critique de Marxism*:

in making the list of references, we find that they are disparate, and that they appear frequently in terms of three different types: a) illustrations from the history of philosophy; b) ... the reminder of the equal treatment of Hegel and Spinoza as 'dead dogs'; c) the recollection of Spinozist 'themes' destined to underscore the importance of the dialectic (for example: the dialectical assertion *omnis determination est negation*).[30]

However, we should not infer from this the limited importance of Spinoza for Marx. We must remember that Spinoza's influence in the history of philosophy, not just on Marx, but on Nietzsche or Heidegger, is characterised by the particular detour, or undercover manner, in which he has been received. Spinoza has had an underground influence: Althusser notes: 'The history of philosophy's repressed Spinozism thus unfolded as a subterranean history acting at *other sites*, in political and religious ideology (deism) and in the sciences, but not on the illuminated stage of visible philosophy.'[31]

It is then possible to risk a hypothesis relative to the hidden Spinozism of Marx. The hypothesis is in a sense risky (since there is no history of influences that would make it possible to verify it): It is 'as if' Spinoza's *Ethics* had furnished Marx with his ontology, or 'as if' Marx had found his first philosophy in Spinoza, and see what effects this produces in the reading of Marx.[32]

---

[27] Tosel, 'Des usages "Marxistes" de Spinoza: Leçon de méthode', 515.
[28] These texts can be found in the first issue of *Cahiers Spinoza* (Paris: Editions Réplique, 1977).
[29] Marx-Engels Gesamtausgabe (MEGA), Introduction, 21.
[30] Benussan, 'Spinozisme', 1082.
[31] Althusser, 'The Object of Capital', in *Reading Capital*, 102.
[32] This hypothesis lies at the basis of the orientation of Althusser's thought. In a comment published in 2001, Pierre Macherey states that Althusser was convinced that the philosophy of Spinoza is the one 'that Marx never had time to write on his own', adding that Althusser saw it as his fundamental mission to 'give Marxism its own philosophy', 'to give Marxism the metaphysics that it deserves'. Macherey, 'Le Dieu Noir de La Mélancholie'.

This hypothesis is supported by the texts: Marx is not the author of a philosophical system (his major works have in common the fact that they are incomplete); there is no development of a philosophical system as the term is generally used, he even explicitly claimed to be escaping from philosophy, producing a non-philosophical or even an anti-philosophical philosophy. Thus the question can be asked as to what extent can we know that there is a *philosophy* of Marx, which is to say *a* philosophy of Marx. The only thing that is certain is that his work has produced considerable effects in or on philosophy, that the discourse and the practice of philosophy have been profoundly and irreversibly disrupted by Marx. To take the measure of this break, and to extend the effects that it continues to produce, would appear to us today to be enough of a justification for continuing to read Marx.[33]

In considering Marx as a major caesura in the history of philosophy, one can arrive at the idea that that history is profoundly marked by such fault lines and fissures that are the products of seismic phenomena of great extent, and which are themselves mirrors of the movement of the grand continents of thought (only clearly visible in their contours from the point of view of a continuous history of philosophy) that go by the names of Descartes, Leibniz, Hobbes, Hume, Kant, or Hegel. Now if Spinoza is undoubtedly the one whose thought bears witness to the greatest upheaval that took place before Marx in the history of modern philosophy (such a fracture takes place before Spinoza only with Machiavelli and, between Spinoza and Marx, with Vico), it is because it systematically and radically challenged the spontaneous and implicit presuppositions of the discourse and practice of philosophy, such as the interiority of subjectivity, the transparency of consciousness, the freedom of the will, the sovereignty of the state, and divine omnipotence. We can then finally and simply propose the hypothesis that in the history of philosophy the fault line named Spinoza communicates with the fault line named Marx, and that the major telluric effects engendered by the first communicate with the second through subterranean and obscure pathways (without a doubt there are other communications with other fault lines, not least those named Machiavelli and Vico).

If the hypothesis of this work produces effects that renew the reading of Marx – if Marx thereby becomes something else, somehow rejuvenated through this hypothesis – we nevertheless do not conclude that Marx was himself a Spinozist. We claim only that Spinoza aids us in being able to read

---

[33] On these points see Étienne Balibar's introduction to *The Philosophy of Marx*.

and comprehend Marx, and that Marx, by going outside of the ruins of the orthodoxies that have claimed him, can be returned to life by Spinoza.[34] In short, it is then perhaps Spinoza who makes Marx actual and thus vibrant.

[34] However, we could say that reading an author by way of a detour through another author is a well-known strategy, especially when it comes to the history of reading Marx through the detour of Spinoza. In terms of these other strategies of the same sort, notably Althusser's proposal to read Marx and Spinoza, our perspective differs in that it consists in demonstrating that it is Marx's texts themselves that demand a detour through Spinoza, which is not then an external hypothesis of interpretation. Attention is paid to Marx's texts in order to demonstrate that the Spinozist detour is to some extent already included and required by them, notably the *1844 Manuscripts*, and that Althusser can be considered still Hegelian or Feuerbachian. We would not want to say that there is an influence of Spinoza on Marx, but that Spinoza produces effects in the text of Marx, which is not the same thing.

2
Pars Naturae

The relation of Marx to Spinoza is articulated around a central thesis that is repeated several times in the 1844 Manuscripts: 'Man lives from nature', 'man is a part of nature',[1] states the first manuscript, while the third is more precise: 'an objective being . . . creates and establishes only objects because it is established by objects, because it is fundamentally nature'; 'man is directly a natural being'.[2] If the determination of man as a natural being can be attributed to Feuerbach, then the idea of humanity as part of nature can be considered to come from Spinoza. This thesis, central to Spinozism in that it signifies the insertion of humanity within the general and common order of nature, thereby ruining humanity's immediate conception of itself as a 'kingdom within a kingdom', is equally central to Marx, and not just to his early writings but as a thesis that is returned to in his later works. Indeed, he returns to the notion in one of his very last writings, 'Notes on Adolph Wagner's "Lehrbuch der politischen Ökonomie"', 'the last and most lovely text' according to Althusser,[3] where he writes: '[human beings] begin, like every animal, by *eating, drinking*, etc., that is not by "finding themselves" in a relationship, but *actively behaving*, availing themselves of certain things of the outside world by action, and thus satisfying their needs. (They start, then, with production.)'[4] In this passage, arguing against 'the natural tendency of a German Professor of Economics' to imagine that the primary relation of man to nature is a theoretical relationship of knowledge and contemplation, Marx insists that the original relationship of human beings to nature is not an external relationship of knowledge but rather a relationship of implica-

[1] Marx, *Early Writings*, 328.
[2] Ibid., 389.
[3] Althusser, 'Marx in his Limits', 37.
[4] Marx, 'Notes on Adolph Wagner's "Lehrbuch der politischen Ökonomie"'.

tion characteristic of a natural being which, insofar as it has needs, begins by being affected by nature and other natural beings. Affects and passivity are thus primary; they engender human activity and a practical relation with nature which is a reaction and response to this original affection.

What exactly does this affirmation of man as a being of nature, as a part of nature, mean for Marx? After all, he did not, or could not, give these formulations a literal Spinozist sense. It means first of all that man is 'objective, natural, and sensuous',[5] that is to say, a finite mode amongst an infinity of other such modes. The determination of humanity as an objective being would be returned to by Marx again and again, up to and including in *Capital*, where he writes that 'the human being itself, considered as a pure existence of labour power, is a natural object, a thing, certainly living and conscious of itself, but a thing – and work properly speaking is a reification of this force'.[6] Adopting the point of view according to which the human being is first of all a being in nature, a thing in the world, is exactly to adopt the Spinozist point of view according to which humans must first be grasped as a finite mode: it is to start, as Spinoza does, from the double fact of knowing, on the one hand, that 'man thinks' and, on the other, that 'we feel that a certain body is affected in many ways'[7] – it being understood that these two traits are at the same level and of equal importance, since the fact that we find ourselves to be thinking our thoughts accompanies the fact that we are aware of our body being affected by other things. Or, as Spinoza puts it: 'if the object of the idea constituting a human mind is a body, nothing can happen in that body which is not perceived by the mind'.[8] In the same way as the affection of the body, thought is a fact of nature, part of the natural being of humanity: thought does not found the exceptional character of humanity in the sense of being something outside of nature. To say that 'man consists of a mind and a body'[9] is to say that, insofar as it is a natural, living and animated being, a human being is a mode of extension, and therefore a body,[10] and that the existence of an idea is the same thing, but considered

---

[5] Marx, *Early Writings*, 389.
[6] Marx, *Capital, Volume I*, 310. Translation modified.
[7] Spinoza, *Ethics* II, Ax. 2 and *Ethics* II Ax. 4; CWS I, 448.
[8] Spinoza, *Ethics* II, 12; CWS I, 456–7.
[9] Spinoza, *Ethics* II, 13 Cor.; CWS I, 457.
[10] Here we must take into consideration the fact that the human being as a mode of extension and thus a body is equally fundamental for Marx: 'The first premise of all human history is, of course, the existence of living human individuals. Thus the first fact to be established is the physical organisation of these individuals and their consequent relation to the rest of nature.' Marx and Engels, *The German Ideology*, 37.

as a mode of thinking rather than extension: 'a mode of extension and the idea of that mode are one and the same thing, but expressed in two ways',[11] so that 'the mind and the body, are one and the same individual, which is conceived now under the attribute of thought, now under the attribute of extension'.[12] To say that human beings think is therefore to say that they are constituted by a mind, and that the mind is at the same time constituted by an idea in which the object is the body of the human. Thus there is nothing exceptional about human beings, since for every existing individual as a mode of extension there is an idea in God, such that it is necessary to say that all bodies or modes of extension are living and animated, 'although to diverse degrees',[13] since they are all minds constituted by the idea in which the object is exactly their body.

'As a natural, corporeal, sensuous, objective being [the human] is a suffering, conditioned, objective being', Marx writes in the *1844 Manuscripts*; '[humanity] is a suffering, conditioned and limited being, like animals and plants'.[14] Which means that insofar as they are part of nature and thus part of the finite world, human beings are not able to escape being subject to the effects of other parts of nature. In Spinoza's terms: 'we are acted on, insofar as we are part of nature, which cannot be conceived through itself without the others'.[15] One can understand, then, how Marx could be led to say that 'man's *feelings*, passions, etc., are not merely anthropological characteristics in the narrower sense, but are truly *ontological* affirmations of his essence'.[16] It is insofar as he is uniquely Spinozist that Marx can think the properly ontological sense of the human passions: their impact is ontological in the sense that they reveal the immersion of humanity in the common order of nature and not as an exception to it. Taking human passions seriously, understanding them as the effects of one part of nature produced by other parts of nature, is thus to recognise the originary passionate servitude of humans insofar they are natural and living beings. At the same time, admitting this anthropological truth, which could be called naturalist, leads to an ontology of essential finitude. This is what Marx recognises more clearly than Feuerbach, because the former is more Spinozist than the latter.

[11] Spinoza, *Ethics* II, 7 Schol.; *CWS* I, 451.
[12] Spinoza, *Ethics* II, 21 Schol.; *CWS* I, 467.
[13] Spinoza, *Ethics* II, 13 Schol.; *CWS* I, 457.
[14] Marx, *Early Writings*, 389. One can see here a criticism addressed to Feuerbach for whom the point of view is limited to an anthropology and not an ontology.
[15] Spinoza, *Ethics* IV, 2; *CWS* I, 548.
[16] Marx, *Early Writings*, 375.

The shared thesis according to which the individual human is part of nature and not in nature as 'a kingdom within a kingdom' brings Spinoza and Marx to a common conclusion: that individual existence is relative, that no individual exists or can be conceived by itself independently of its relationships to other parts of nature. The relational character of the parts of nature is decisive here: conceived as a part of nature, and as itself composed of elements which are equally parts of nature, an individual or a singular being can no longer be conceived as possessing a closed or substantial identity. A singular individual must be understood to be at the same time relative both to the parts that make it up and to the greater ensemble of which it is a part. In other words, it is only a relatively and momentarily individualised being, since its individual existence comes from the ensemble of its relations with other parts of nature, an ensemble that is provisionally stabilised in such a way as to permit the emergence, in itself contingent, of such a singular individual.

As a part of nature, the human individual can only be conceived of relationally. It must be added that this is increasingly true of those natural individuals whose bodies are made up of more parts than others, and of those capable of entering into a greater number of relationships with other parts of nature.[17] This point is equally fundamental for Marx when he writes, in the 'Theses on Feuerbach', that the 'essence of man' is an 'ensemble of social relations'.[18] It is correct that this conception of the individual human as part of nature leads Marx as much as Spinoza to affirm that human beings are naturally social (and not just naturally sociable). Although human beings are 'usually envious and burdensome to one another', Spinoza writes, '[t]hey can hardly ... live a solitary life; hence, that definition which makes man a social animal has been quite pleasing to most. And surely we do derive, from the society of our fellow men, many more advantages than disadvantages.'[19] In a famous passage from the Introduction to the *Grundrisse* (known as the 1857 Introduction), Marx writes: 'The human being is in the most literal sense a political animal [ζῶον πολιτιχόν], not merely a gregarious animal, but an animal which can individuate itself only in the midst of society';[20] and more radically still in the larger body of the *Grundrisse*: 'human beings become individuals only through the process of history. He appears originally

---

[17] Here we can see that the negation of the extraordinary nature of humanity neither limits comprehension of the specificity of humanity nor attributes to it an ensemble of particular characteristics.
[18] Marx, *Early Writings*, 423.
[19] Spinoza, *Ethics* IV, 35 Schol.; CWS I, 563.
[20] Marx, *Grundrisse*, 84.

as species-being [Gattungswesen], clan being, herd animal – although in no way whatever as ζῶον πολιτιχόν in the political sense.'[21] But if the human being is an animal that can only individuate itself in society this signifies also that the individuation of human beings is all the greater in those social relations that are the most numerous and developed: it is solely in the historical epochs of the greatest development of social relations (notably under the form of commodity exchange) that human beings can conceive of themselves as self-sufficient, or, as Marx calls them, not without irony, 'isolated individuals'. It is the same development of these social relations that leads individuals to a conception of themselves as isolated individuals, as autonomous and self-sufficient subjects. It is therefore the entire history of the development of social relations that produces this inversion by which human beings, originally parts of nature and things in nature, come to see themselves as the exact opposite of that which they are, to know themselves as subjects substantially different from things, as subjects that reign sovereignly over nature and not as objective beings that are part of nature.

---

[21] Ibid., 496.

3
Enduring Social Relations

The way in which Spinoza initially poses the social nature of humanity in the Scholia of Proposition 35 of Part IV of the *Ethics* can at first appear troubling: although people are most often a nuisance to each other, nevertheless, Spinoza explains, most are not able to live solitary lives and have need of others. Everything transpires as if human beings admit their nature as social animals as a kind of concession: you have make do with others, deal with them, even if deep down you cannot help but harbour a secret hope of doing without them. Humanity would thus be such that its social nature appears to be a nuisance – something that, even as part of its essence, takes the form of a constraint that must be endured, since one cannot make do without it and must make the best of a bad hand. In short, at first sight, human beings have a bad consciousness of their own nature as social and socialised beings. This is derived from the fact that, if human beings, insofar as they are essentially part of nature, are beings in and through the relations they enter into with other parts of nature, and notably with other people, those relations are primarily relations that they endure.[1] In other words, the passions are not understood by Spinoza to be the antithesis of sociality, as a rebellious element that must be tamed and disciplined in order to institute sociality; on the contrary, the passions are in themselves and by themselves sociality. There is certainly the possibility of socialising through reason,[2] but, *here and now*, the fact is that it is not by reason that human beings are socialised,

---

[1] One finds confirmation of this point in Pierre Macherey's study 'Spinoza, the End of History, and the Ruse of Reason', 155.

[2] Reason is even by far the most reliable principle of socialisation: 'insofar as men live according to the guidance of reason, they must do only those things which are good for human nature . . . and each man . . . Hence, insofar as men live according to the guidance of reason, they must always agree among themselves.' Spinoza, *Ethics* IV, 35 Dem.; *CWS* I, 563.

but through the passions, and this to the extent that passionate life is, like reason, engendered in each person by their effort to persevere in their being. The passions (joy and sadness, love and hate, hope and fear) socialise just as much and more surely than reason, the only difference being that socialisation through the passions does not lead human beings to the necessary mutual accord, but actually leads them to the reverse, to a social life marked by conflict and opposition. Being powerless in common is still a manner of being assembled and making society: it is the actual manner in which human beings are in fact made into society.

Here we find a terrain of agreement between Marx and Spinoza. For Spinoza, people are always initially socialised by affects, and more particularly by the sad affects, and therefore the passions, notably the fundamental passions of hope and fear. If their socialisation is made primarily through the passions, and is therefore passive, it is natural that human beings should initially have a negative awareness of their nature as social animals, and that socialisation be imposed on them as a painful constraint that they inevitably begin by simply enduring. That social relations are initially endured follows inevitably from the fact that 'human beings are necessarily subject to affections',[3] that is to say, that they find themselves placed in a relation with others (as with other parts of nature) on the negative basis of passive affect (pity, envy, hope, fear, vengeance). But the primary character of affective dependency and of passivity follows necessarily from the nature of humanity as a part of nature: passivity and being a part of nature are one and the same thing.

For Marx, it is equally true that social relations are always initially something human beings endure rather than will; that is to say, they are relations in which human beings experience their lack of power (individual as much as collective) and not their proper activity.[4] 'The reality which communism creates', Marx and Engels write, 'is precisely the true basis for rendering it impossible that anything should exist independently of individuals, insofar as reality is nevertheless only a product of the preceding intercourse (*Verkehr*) of individuals.'[5] So individuals are initially related to the conditions of their own existence as natural conditions in the sense that these conditions are imposed upon them, are endured without having been chosen; these condi-

---

[3] Spinoza, TP I, 4; CWS II, 505.

[4] Need we be reminded that for Spinoza to be active and to be led by reason are one and the same thing? 'Human beings are only active insofar as they are led by reason.' Spinoza, *Ethics* IV, 35; CWS I, 563.

[5] Marx and Engels, *The German Ideology*, 90. Translation modified.

tions thus also remain exterior. At first glance, people consider as natural, and therefore as simply given, conditions that have actually been produced and fostered by previous generations. Communism, says Marx, creates or works to create conditions that will make it impossible for human beings to relate to the social and historical conditions of their existence as conditions that are simply endured by them and thus are independent from and external to them. 'Communism . . . for the first time consciously treats all natural premises as the creations of hitherto existing men, strips them of their natural character and subjugates them to the power of the united individuals.'[6] It is an act of transformation, both in practice and in and through theory, that makes it possible for people to comprehend that their social conditions and their existence are produced and engendered socially by other people, and therefore that their relation to these conditions is susceptible to being socially and collectively mastered, dominated and eventually modified and transformed by them.

In Marx and Engels' assertion that 'communists treat the conditions created by production and commerce before them as inorganic factors',[7] the term 'inorganic' must be taken in the sense that Marx gives it in the *1844 Manuscripts*: 'Nature is man's inorganic body – nature, that is, insofar as is not the human body';[8] and additionally in the *Grundrisse*: 'just as the working subject appears naturally as an individual, as natural being – so does the first objective condition of his labour appear as nature, earth, as his inorganic body'.[9] What Marx calls 'inorganic' or 'non-organic' here is not something that could be described as mechanical; it is rather that which prolongs the organic body of the individual, and with which the individual makes part of his body in the deployment of his own activity. Treating the conditions engendered by human production anterior to us as the organic conditions of our proper existence – that is, as conditions that our existence prolongs or is prolonged through – is thus to treat them as something that we have the capacity to master, as conditions we can dispose of, rather than as something that is imposed on us as a natural given, radically independent of us and exterior to us. Of course, as a Spinozist, Marx would not want to say that past generations of humans consciously made that which has become the conditions of our existence. This would be to return to the illusion of final causes, which Marx was on guard against lapsing into: 'the communists do

---

[6] Ibid.
[7] Ibid.
[8] Marx, *Early Writings*, 328.
[9] Marx, *Grundrisse*, 488.

not imagine that it was the plan or destiny of previous generations to give them material'.[10] Previous generations did not themselves already know the non-organic conditions for our existence (they knew only the conditions they themselves endured); they could not engender our conditions with the awareness that the conditions they produced would or could become organic conditions for us.

Considering 'all prior natural conditions as the creation of the people who have come before us' – and therefore not as natural in the sense of a given which is imposed upon us and that we must endure, but as the product of a previous human activity susceptible of being the support of our activity – is certainly to consider these conditions as socially engendered. But it is also and consequently to take the position that we do not always have to suffer these conditions, and that therefore a liberation from a purely *imaginary* perception of these conditions is possible. For Spinoza, social relations are imaginary to the same extent that they are always relations founded on and by the affects: the imaginary character of social relations is the consequence of a socialisation that always takes place primarily through the affects or passions. Social relations are initially imaginary because they are endured, and they are endured because they are passions. These social relations that individuals are subjected to are imagined as external by the very same individuals that enter into them; by virtue of this exteriority these relations take on the aspect of a natural given that is indifferent to individuals and is suffered by them. While in a certain sense agreeing with Spinoza that social relations are always initially relations that are endured, Marx puts more emphasis on their exteriority than on their affective dimension. That is, for Marx, as much as these relations are suffered, they always take the form of an activity: they are 'relations of production' and as such indissociable from a certain historical state of the productive forces. 'The relation between productive forces and the form of exchange', Marx and Engels explain, 'is the relationship between the form of exchange and the activity (*Tätigkeit*) or the activation (*Betätigung*) of individuals.'[11] Marx considers human individuals to be first and foremost always already active, and to be so to the extent that they are individually human – which is to say that what distinguishes them from nonhuman living things is how they 'produce their means of existence'.[12] Marx insists on the fact that this activity is not solely one in which individuals reproduce conditions of existence that are already given, conditions

---

[10] Marx and Engels, *The German Ideology*, 90. Translation modified.
[11] Ibid. Translation modified.
[12] Ibid., 42.

that permit them to reproduce or maintain their existence; individuals do not act solely to reproduce their existence but also to engender and produce new means of existence that are irreducible to the natural existence already given. For Marx, human beings do more than just affirm their existence; they distinguish themselves immediately from other natural beings in they do not manifest solely an activity of simple perseverance in their existence: insofar as they are human individuals, they are not content to simply desire, conserve, maintain and reproduce the given conditions that make possible their existence; rather, they produce new means of existence beyond what is simply given. They are human, according to Marx and Engels, in that they are always already active and productive: 'As individuals express their life, so they are'; '[w]hat they are, therefore, coincides with their production, both with what they produce and with how they produce'.[13] This is a conception to which Spinoza would also be quick to subscribe because what he calls the conatus is not a simple activity of conserving existence or reproducing the existing conditions that make existence possible; rather, the conatus is the positive affirmation of an active power that does not exhaust itself in maintaining the existing conditions of existence, but endeavours to increase or amplify this existence – which certainly cannot take place without engendering new conditions of existence that make possible a greater affirmation and a more intense existence. '[T]he power of natural things, by which they exist and have effects, is the very power of God . . .',[14] and this power being infinite it appears that the conatus cannot just preserve life but must also amplify and intensify it, which requires going beyond the current conditions of life, conditions that may permit the conservation of life but not the augmentation of the power to act.

Marx and Spinoza necessarily face the same difficulty: how to reconcile the definition of natural things, including human beings, by their power to act and by their natural tendency to augment this power with the recognition that the primary relations that these same beings are subjected to are relations that they are passively subjected to? How to affirm at the same time the fact that human beings are socialised by affects that are primarily passions – that they are inevitably led by a social life that they undergo, by which they are rendered passive – and the fact that human beings are

---

[13] Ibid., 43.
[14] Spinoza, *TP* II, 3; *CWS* II, 507. See also *Ethics* IV, 4 Dem.; *CWS* I, 548–9: 'The power by which singular things (and consequently [any] man) preserve their being is the power itself of God, or Nature not insofar as it is infinite, but insofar as it can be explained through the man's actual essence.'

originally active and productive (Marx), or that they tend naturally not only to the conservation of their being but also to the augmentation of their power to act (Spinoza)? If the desires of human beings are first determined by appetite and not by reason, and if, therefore, 'their natural power or right must be defined not by reason but by any appetite by which they may be determined to act', then Spinoza admits that 'in the case of those desires that do not arise from reason, men are not so much active as passive'.[15] If desire is just another name for the effort that each takes in conserving its being and augmenting its power to act, then it is necessary to say that it is under the form of the passions that this capacity to act is deployed. The apparent contradiction is sublimated by the emphasis that is placed, as in Spinoza, on the perspective of 'the universal power of nature': whether a human being acts according to its proper nature and the function of its own utility (which could be called conduct by reason), or whether it acts by being determined by something else, in each case it is a matter of 'the natural force by which a man follows those things that promote his preservation'.[16] Passivity only exists as something relative to the individual considered, or to a finite existing mode for which it would signify a reduction of its activity, a separation from its power of acting: a passive individual or an individual rendered passive is determined by something other than itself to produce an effect, but this effect, moreover, is made up perfectly by its cause. This cause is not the singular individual in question, and the effect produced is not explained by its power to act but by the power of something other, by a power that passes through it, traversing the individual, but not starting with it. In other words, passivity absolutely does not exist from the entirely positive and infinitely affirmative point of view of nature itself,[17] in which the power and infinite activity also expresses itself in human affects and passions, and is equally expressed in our inadequate ideas which are imaginations; God or nature is positively the cause of our inadequate ideas to the extent that God is affected not just by the idea of our body but also by the idea of a great number of other bodies.[18] In brief, far from seeing passivity as bad, it can only be said to be so from the determined and particular point of view of an existing mode, which calls 'bad' that which is simply a nuisance from its point of view, and 'passivity' that which cannot be explained by its own power of acting, that is to say, which separates

---

[15] Spinoza, *TP* II, 5; *CWS* II, 508.
[16] Spinoza, *Ethics* II, 9 Schol.; *CWS* I, 500. Translation modified.
[17] Spinoza, *Ethics* II, 45 Schol.; *CWS* I, 482.
[18] Spinoza, *Ethics* II, 33 and 35; *CWS* I, 472.

it from that power, or more exactly from its limit, which it reduces and diminishes.

If we return to Marx, it seems that we now touch on a point from which it would no longer be possible to pursue our parallel reading of the two philosophers. On the side of Spinoza we have a thought which only knows affirmation and for which all negation, all negativity, is only thinkable from the point of view of an existing finite mode; the attributes constitute the essence of substance only to the extent that they are nothing other than the absolute and infinite affirmation, but the attributes only affirm the essence of substance in that they also affirm the modes whose essences they contain: in brief, for Spinoza, being or existing is that which can only affirm itself and affirm that which exists. There is no place for negation here, as Deleuze notes when he writes that 'Spinoza's philosophy is a philosophy of pure affirmation', and that 'affirmation is the speculative principle on which the entirety of the *Ethics* depends'.[19] With Marx, on the contrary, we have a thinker who can be called a 'dialectician' only in that his thought reserves a place for negation and the negative in general, and more precisely to the extent that he conceives of affirmation not as an immediately affirmative action but as the act of negating the negative. Here one finds the irreducibly Hegelian heritage of Marx, and therefore reaches that point beyond which it would no longer be possible to pursue a parallel reading of Marx and Spinoza. Thus it would be tempting to see, as one possible example, negativity as the permanent condition that would make Marx's thought a philosophy of history, and, inversely, to see the absence of the negative in Spinoza as the reason for the at least apparent difficulty of thinking history from a Spinozist point of view.

This point is therefore decisive and it can only be examined concretely starting from the principal form that the negative takes with respect to Marx, namely the form of contradiction and its role in the Marxist concept of history. It is here that we encounter anew Althusser's thought. From our perspective, Althusser's major contribution resides in his no longer reading Marx as a Hegelian: if Marx is the greatest of the young Hegelians, it is because he is the only one who did not remain a Hegelian. Starting from Kant and Fichte before comprehending the thought of Hegel 'von Anfang bis Ende' (from the beginning to the end),[20] Marx had at one and the same time an exceptional understanding of Hegel's thought and sufficient distance such that he could be Hegelian while at same time taking leave from that

---

[19] Deleuze, *Expressionism in Philosophy*, 60. Translation modified.
[20] According to Marx in his letter to his father of 10 November 1837.

thought.²¹ This is what permits him, in his maturity, to be fair to Hegel and not 'treat him as a dead dog', and is also what saves us from having to posit a definitive 'break' between a still-Hegelian Marx and a Marx who would no longer be Hegelian. Positing a non-Hegelian Marx makes it necessary to face the difficulty posed by those concepts in Marx that maintain at least the appearance of a Hegelian heritage – of which the concept of contradiction would certainly be the principal instance (to the extent that it implies the others: negativity, negation of the negation, dialectical moment, sublation, i.e. *Aufhebung*). Althusser understood this well, and it was the reason he elaborated a theory of the 'overdetermined contradiction'²² to demonstrate that the Marxist contradiction is no longer the Hegelian contradiction (for us the problem is that this demonstration is derived more from Lenin and Mao than from Marx himself). Is such an anti-Hegelianism really enough to make the claim – as we do here – that Marx is a Spinozist? To say, in effect, that there is only position and affirmation, that the actual can only be an affirmation?²³ Would not the rational point of view with respect to Hegel also be the point of view of absolute affirmation and full positivity? The contradiction would only be valid in Hegel's own thought from the point of view that he considers 'rationally negative', that is to say the point of view of an immediate negation of the negativity of the understanding, a negation which must itself still be negated in order to be made correct or rational, which is to say positive and affirmative, which are, by definition the only actual reality. For Hegel, however, the access to the rational (i.e., it is only the affirmation of totality that is true) takes place under the form

---

[21] The 1843 Kreuznach Manuscript (*Critique of Hegel's Philosophy of Right*) is where Marx's thought is able to inscribe itself in Hegel's text while at the same time taking its distance from it and writing against it.

[22] See Althusser, 'Contradiction and Overdetermination (Notes for an Investigation)' and 'On the Materialist Dialectic (On the Unevenness of Origins)', in *For Marx*. On this point see note 50 on page 217, where Althusser recognises the disconcerting aspect of a Marxist dialectic that dispenses with alienation, negativity, negation of the negation, *Aufhebung*, etc.

[23] This would lead us to the point of view, with respect to Marx, to the idea that a contradiction is not evidence of the reality and active existence (effectivity) of the negative at the heart of what exists, but that, thus constituted, it is the product of an *a posteriori* explication and a retrospective reconstruction of historical change. To clarify, we are not saying that there is no concept of contradiction in Marx but that his concept of contradiction does not imply negation. A contradiction in Marx is always the effective encounter of two tendencies affirming themselves as opposed, effectively a struggle of one against the other in a relationship that does not consist of one negating the other than in subjugating it.

of an admission that gives every part of the totality its own finitude, which must be surmounted by conceiving and constituting its own 'ideality', that is to say its non-actuality: there is nothing like this in either Spinoza or Marx, who are thinkers of finitude not simply as something that exists, but as something that is also affirmed as such,[24] rightfully considered to be a real and actual part of the totality, and not that which exists only to be negated. The non-idealism of Spinoza and Marx consists precisely in their refusal of the ideality of the finite, and therefore in the thesis that makes the finite part of the totality a fully positive existence that is nothing other than the totality insofar as it is expressed in the part.

---

[24] Concerning Spinoza, see the demonstration of this point by Jean-Marie Vaysse in his book *Totalité et Finitude: Heidegger et Spinoza*.

4

The Identity of Nature and History[1]

In a text from 1961 titled 'The Quest for the Meaning of History', which appeared as an appendix to his major work *Welgeschichte un Heilgeschehen* (*Meaning and History: The Theological Implications of the Philosophy of History*), Karl Löwith interrogates the modern dislocation of the 'unitary and total world split into two different worlds': on the one side the world of nature and on the other the historical world, an ontological separation which is doubled in an epistemological separation between 'the world of modern science and a historical human world, the world of the humanities'.[2] As might be expected, Löwith repeats the claim that the role of the founder of the first world is Descartes, while, for the second world, he repeats the claim that its founder is Vico, adding that, 'at the end of this split between nature and history, there stands the assertion of Hegel's pupil, Marx, that "history is the true natural history of man"'.[3] In the commentary he offers on this famous formula from the *1844 Manuscripts*, Löwith explains that Marx's thesis is that the world of human beings is not the natural world, that the natural world for humanity is the world of history, that the world is not found by humanity as a natural given, but is produced by humanity and engendered in its work. If that is what Marx had wanted to say, then, on the one hand, we can understand how Löwith makes it the culmination of the modern dissociation of nature and history, and on the other, why it is then possible to cite Dilthey after Marx, making them part of the same tra-

---

[1] This chapter is a revised and modified version of a text originally titled 'Vie naturelle et vie historique chez Marx', first published as an article in Number 23 (titled *Penser la vie* and edited by Pierre Montebello) of the review *Kairos* (Presses Universitaires du Mirail, Toulouse, 2004).
[2] Löwith, 'The Quest for the Meaning of History', 140.
[3] Ibid.

jectory:[4] in substance, Marx would not have said anything different from the idealist philosophy of history that preceded him (the Hegelian philosophy of history), nor from the idealist philosophy of the historical life that succeeded him, namely Dilthey's philosophy of the historical science of spirit. From Hegel to Dilthey, passing through Marx, it would then be the same break of nature and history that is accomplished and radicalised. We hope to demonstrate here that this vision of things dissolves the originality of Marx's thought. The materialist conception of history developed by Marx consists not in a repetition of the break between nature and history, as Löwith argues, but in a radical break with this separation that Marx considers to be typical of idealist philosophy. The force of this critique, according to us, lies in its clear understanding of the origin and causes of the *idealist* separation of nature and history and of its *ideological* character. How can Löwith claim that Marx, as a thinker for whom 'history has become everything',[5] for whom it is a matter of humanity finding its 'own meaning in the world of history', 'thereby forgets that historically existing man is only in the world because the world of nature produced him'?[6] If there is such an abstraction in Marx it does not proceed from such a forgetting: it is rather, as Marx states with respect to Feuerbach, that what the philosophers call 'nature' has for a long time been the product of human history; that work, production and 'the material creation of human beings' are 'the basis of the sensible world'. Marx and Engels take care to specify that 'the priority of external nature remains unassailed, and all this has no application to the original men produced by *generatio aequivoca* (spontaneous generation)'. They refuse to consider 'man . . . as distinct from nature'.[7] Generated by and within a nature which pre-exists it, humanity brings with it a specific and particular relation, but the analysis of this relation, which Marx is dedicated to, is never a matter of making it disappear or of dissolving 'the primacy of external nature' in a historically produced second nature, thereby forgetting the latter's secondary status which, on the contrary, Marx considers to be irreducible.

What preserves Marx from a hypostasis of historicity is, as we have already seen, precisely his Spinozism. If there is a philosophy that does not know the opposition between nature and history and which resists positing their separation, it is the philosophy of Spinoza. Not just because for Spinoza there is no real difference between nature and history, but also because for Spinoza it

---

[4] Ibid.
[5] Ibid., 141.
[6] Ibid., 140.
[7] Marx and Engels, *The German Ideology*, 46.

is difficult to even hope to understand history if one isolates it from the general order of nature. If the actors of history are certainly peoples and states, the latter are nonetheless first and foremost made up of natural individuals, subject as such to natural necessity. If history is the history of states, then the history of a state is the history of its formation, development, dissolution and disappearance as a result of internal dissensions and other seditions. In other words, for Spinoza in his *Political Treatise*, there is a knowledge of nature that makes possible the understanding of history, a nature that makes history intelligible. History consists of nothing other than the natural effort that human beings expend in order to create their collective power, to create the conditions that increase this power, and of the causes (equally natural) which in contradicting this effort thereby return human beings to their native impotence. We can therefore say, following Étienne Balibar, that for Spinoza 'nature . . . is nothing other than a new way of thinking about history, according to a method of rational exegesis that seeks to explain events by their causes'.[8] Historical knowledge cannot be of a different order to natural knowledge for the reason that the actors of history are themselves nothing other than things in nature, parts of nature. If the dualism of nature and history, of the natural world and human history, is, as Löwith argues, the dualism typical of modernity, then it is necessary to state that Spinoza is a notable exception to this. He is not, however, the only one: Marx is another. That one can find in the knowledge of nature the principles of the intelligibility of history: this is the basic hypothesis common to Spinoza and Marx.

The attention Marx gives to historical human activity, to the human activity of the transformation of nature, never leads him to hypostatise this activity, to make it an activity *sui generis* by which human beings, in affirming themselves as historical beings, insert between themselves and nature the mediation of production, and the social relations of production tear themselves away from nature in instituting a properly human world, a world of history, the significance of which would be that it is substantially different from the natural world.[9] Historical human activity – social activity

---

[8] Balibar, *Spinoza and Politics*, 36.
[9] To a question, formulated in a Kantian fashion, that asks 'under what conditions is history itself possible?', or 'under what conditions is it possible to give signification to the concept of history?', or 'under what conditions is a science of history (according to the expression of *The German Ideology*) possible?', Marx responds that the first condition is to not separate history from nature, nor the history of humanity from the history of nature. This response is diametrically opposed to the answer given by the neo-Kantian tradition (which in the broad sense includes Dilthey) to the same question. Cassirer responds that 'when compared to the objects of natural science the objects of histor-

in the form of 'industry' and 'commerce' – remains always for Marx a sensible, material and natural form of activity consisting of 'the production and exchange of vital needs'.[10] Far from being an activity that would engender a world the significance of which would lie in its independence from or opposition to nature, the human activity of production, as social and historical activity, is for Marx the specifically human modality that affirms the manifest unity of humanity and nature. Marx's point of departure is the Feuerbachian thesis of this unity, but rethought as an active unity, a productive process, wherein the defining quality of the natural being of humanity is its ability to transform its 'vital living milieu' into a 'social milieu', which does not thereby cease to be any less 'vital' and therefore natural.[11]

The interpretation of the Marxist philosophy of history we find in Löwith is evidence of the current resistance to understanding 'that the celebrated "unity of man with nature" has always existed in industry and has existed in varying forms in every epoch according to the lesser or greater development of industry'.[12] This analysis would only be complete on the condition that it also demonstrates the resistance to elevating the concepts of 'industry' and 'production' to the dignity of major philosophical concepts that make it possible to understand human activity as being at once vital and social, as the identity of nature and history.

In *The German Ideology*, Marx and Engels make the following very clear remarks concerning the question of the articulation of nature and history: 'We know only a single science, the science of history. One can look at history from two sides and divide it into the history of nature and the history of men. The two sides are, however, inseparable; the history of nature and the history of men are dependent on each other so long as men exist.'[13]

---

ical science seem to be much more fugitive and evanescent', identifying this added dimension as the symbolic dimension (Cassirer, 'The Philosophy of History', 138). In refusing any distinctions between nature and history, between 'physics' and the 'symbolic', Marx also excludes, on the epistemological terrain, any difference of method between the sciences of nature and the historical sciences. But more important than any of this is that he situates the natural and historical (and therefore social) origin of this idealistic type of distinction and demonstrates its ideological character.

[10] Marx and Engels, *The German Ideology*, 49.
[11] The expressions 'vital living milieu' (*körperliches Lebensmedium*) and 'vital social milieu' (*soziales Lebensmedium*) are not Marx's but derive originally from Moses Hess, who used them in his text *Sur l'essence de l'argent*, which had a huge influence on Marx when he was writing the *1844 Manuscripts*.
[12] Marx and Engels, *The German Ideology*, 45.
[13] Ibid., 34.

At first glance, a declaration of this sort might seem to give credibility to Löwith's interpretation: Marx explains clearly that his point of view is absolutely and radically historical. The distinction he articulates, however, is not a distinction between nature and history, but between the history of nature and the history of men: the fact that humanity has a history or is a historical species does not imply that it escapes nature or the natural order, for the simple reason that nature itself has a history or is itself already historical. The history of humanity is itself already inscribed in the history of nature, such that, according to the *1844 Manuscripts*, 'History itself is a real part of natural history and of nature's becoming man.'[14] Moreover, as Marx and Engels explain in the passage cited above, the two histories, natural and human, 'are not separable'. It is necessary to take very seriously this affirmation of the inseparability of history and nature: it signifies that there is no historical fact that is not also a natural fact, but also reciprocally (and this reciprocity is difficult to understand) that every natural fact is a historical fact. Thus, in *The German Ideology*, it is clear that what Marx and Engels call 'the first historical act' is also at the same time a natural fact: 'The first historical act is thus the production of the means to satisfy these needs,[15] the production of material life itself.'[16] It is necessary to be attentive to the precise terms used here: the German text states 'die erste geschichtliche Tat'; this signifies that the first historical fact is an act (*Tat*), consistent with the material activity by which human beings produce the conditions permitting them to maintain and perpetuate their life. The first historical act is therefore the natural activity that human beings deploy in satisfying the needs that are theirs insofar they are part of nature as well. But why qualify this act as a historical act? Why does this activity that is work, which is perfectly natural, make history? We would be totally wrong if we answered by saying that it is the act by which human beings tear themselves away from nature and assert themselves as historical beings. The act of producing the material conditions of life does not rip humanity from the realm of nature, since there are other species of animals which also naturally produce the conditions that allow them to live. Marx always reminds us that work and production are activities that are themselves perfectly natural: 'labour is, first of all, a process between man and nature, a process by which man, through his own actions, mediates, regulates and controls the metabolism between

---

[14] Marx, *Early Writings*, 355.
[15] Needs, enumerated in the previous sentence, such as 'eating and drinking, a habitation, clothing and many other things'. Marx and Engels, *The German Ideology*, 47.
[16] Ibid., 58.

himself and nature'.[17] Labour is first an 'expression of life',[18] that is to say, an activity of the living, of a naturally living being that mobilises itself and applies itself to a given natural reality of forces that are themselves natural. Marx writes in *Capital* that 'when man engages in production he can only proceed as nature does herself, i.e. he can only change the form of the materials. Furthermore, even in this work of modification he is constantly helped by natural forces.'[19] This clearly states that labour, insofar as it is a specifically human activity of production of use values, does not break with nature and institute a *sui generis* order of things. On the contrary, labour is inscribed in perfect continuity with nature; first because it proceeds by nature (not however by imitation, but because it pursues and continues the natural process of the modification of forms and imposes forms on matter), and then because it mobilises the natural forces of the living while at the same time using the natural forces already at work, as mechanical and chemical forces, within nature itself. Human labour does not create substantially new realities, it acts only to transform a natural and material substrate already present, modifying only its form. However, Marx insists that nature itself does not produce otherwise: it is not materially creative, it is only formally inventive and creative, it invents forms in combining pre-existing materials.

This faculty of using natural forces in order to apply them to and modify a given nature is itself a faculty that human beings share with other living things. *Capital* mentions the work of the spider and the bee, and the *1844 Manuscripts* that of bees, beavers and ants, but in these texts Marx distinguishes animal production from the production of humans and determines what constitutes the latter's unique property. Human beings share with other living things a vital activity of production, to the same extent that they share with them the productive essence of life itself. It is not therefore productive activity itself that distinguishes human beings from animals. Marx continues to maintain this in one of the last texts he writes, the 'Notes on Adolph Wagner's "Lehrbuch der politischen Ökonomie"': human beings 'begin, like every animal, by *eating, drinking,* etc., that is not by "finding themselves" in a relationship, but *actively behaving,* availing themselves of certain things of the outside world by action, and thus satisfying their needs. (They start, then, with production.)'[20] It is therefore not the active and

---

[17] Marx, *Capital, Volume I*, 283.
[18] The concept of *Lebensäusserung* (expression of life) is utilised by Marx in the *1844 Manuscripts* and is also found in the *Grundrisse* where it is applied to the relation between the worker and his work.
[19] Marx, *Capital, Volume I*, 133.
[20] Marx, 'Notes on Adolph Wagner's "Lehrbuch der politischen Ökonomie"'.

productive comportment that distinguishes human beings as such, since this comportment is proper to living beings in general. As are all living things, human beings are originally in the world actively and productively: their first relation to the world is not that of 'subjects' who 'find themselves' facing an objective world, but that of living things who insert themselves actively and productively in the midst of a natural milieu that they essentially depend upon. If productive activity is not in itself specifically human, then human beings can only be distinguished from other living things by their proper modality of production, by a particular modification of productive activity which is in itself part of life itself and of nature in general. As with all natural and living beings, human beings produce, but they produce in different and distinct manner. 'Men can be distinguished from animals by consciousness, by religion or anything else you like', Marx and Engels write in *The German Ideology*, adding that '[t]hey . . . begin to distinguish themselves from animals as soon as they begin to produce their means of subsistence, a step which is conditioned by their physical organization'.[21] Vital and productive activity becomes specifically human from the moment it is no longer oriented only towards immediate needs but engenders means that make it possible to satisfy other needs: productive activity is human when it mediates the articulation of needs. This activity is made possible by the delay and deferment of the immediate satisfaction of needs that finally makes possible new means that will satisfy more and better needs.[22] Marx is quite clear that it is this supplemental relation to nature that human beings introduce and that other living beings ignore: for human beings 'nature is first a means of immediate subsistence' but, 'second, it is the matter, the object and tool of its life activity'.[23] The first relation to nature is not properly human, and human beings have it in common with other living things. The second relation, on the other hand, is unique to them: it consists in seeing nature not just as a pantry (which it always remains for animals), as a storehouse of means of subsistence, or as their 'original larder',[24] as Max puts it in *Capital*, but also as an arsenal of tools, or, according to another expression from *Capital*, as a 'original tool house' and therefore as a stockpile of instruments capable of being utilised for specific ends. The specific relation of human beings

---

[21] Marx and Engels, *The German Ideology*, 37.

[22] By focusing on the means of satisfaction rather than immediately on satisfaction itself, the productive activity becomes strictly speaking 'work': Marx maintains the Hegelian characterisation of work as 'desire held in check, fleetingness staved off' (Hegel, *Phenomenology of Spirit*, 118).

[23] Marx, *Early Writings*, 328.

[24] Marx, *Capital, Volume I*, 285

to nature is one of utilising things in nature, and nature in its entirety, as they already utilise that portion of nature that is originally nearby as their own bodies, making 'all of nature their inorganic body'.[25] Human beings produce the means of their existence rather than just allow life to be productive through them, as it is in every other living thing; they are living things in and through which the productivity of life is 'doubled' as an object and thus can be willed as such.[26] In human beings the productivity of life becomes the voluntary production of the means of this productivity; on this basis, human production makes possible an unprecedented increase in the very productivity of life. This also signifies that in humanity the natural productivity of nature arrives at knowledge of itself, that is to say at self-consciousness, becoming the activity by which it wills and engenders the means of its own accumulation.

From the *1844 Manuscripts* up to *Capital*, Marx characterises the natural activity of humanity by the fact that it is a generic activity (according to the Feuerbachian and Hessian vocabulary employed by Marx in 1844), that is to say a conscious activity: 'the animal', he writes in the *1844 Manuscripts*, 'is immediately one with its live activity. It is its live activity. Man makes his life activity itself the object of his will and of his consciousness.'[27] Humanity is not only its vital productive activity; it possesses it, has it as an object, and knows itself as itself, and through this activity it takes consciousness of itself. The being or essence of its vital activity is for humanity an object: this is what makes it a generic activity, an activity of which human beings become conscious, and which also enables them to recognise the products of this activity as being properly theirs. In *Capital*, Marx states the same thing when he writes, 'what distinguishes the worst architect from the best of bees is that the architect builds the cell in his mind before he constructs it in wax'.[28] The consequence of this consciousness of the end of production is that a natural given can be utilised and then transformed in order to function as the means to realise this end: 'nature becomes one of the organs of his activity, which he annexes to his own bodily organs, adding stature to himself in spite of the Bible'.[29] So it is only with humanity that vital activity can be properly considered productive:[30] it is productive in the sense that it engenders

---

[25] Marx, *Early Writings*, 328.
[26] We will try to specify the sense of 'doubling' (*Verdopplung*) in what follows.
[27] Ibid.
[28] Marx, *Capital, Volume I*, 284.
[29] Ibid., 285.
[30] In this sense, natural productive activity becomes with human beings the activity of producers, or, better still, the natural productivity becomes human production: this

the object in which the agent can recognise him or herself to the extent that he or she is conscious of its products. There is an actual production when there is, on the one hand, the creation of products that are actually exterior to the producer (that are in fact actual objects), and when, on the other hand, the producer knows them to be their proper production. The question of whether humanity is productive because it is conscious or conscious because it is productive would certainly be in Marx's eyes a false problem (this is why he does not pose it); he says simply that '[t]he practical creation of an objective world, the fashioning of inorganic nature, is proof that man is a conscious species-being';[31] in other words, what matters is the manner in which humanity proves itself to be a species-being; it is in the activity by which it proves itself that it becomes conscious of its own essence. The question of knowing if it would be a conscious being independent of the activity by which it manifests itself is an absurd question since it would be tantamount to asking if it would be in itself that which it only is in being for itself. It is necessary simply to say that production (as an activity that engenders objective products and the elaboration of an objective world) is the space of a 'doubling' (*Verdoppelung*) that permits the self-attestation of the agent insofar as it is conscious of its species essence: work can therefore be qualified as a 'species-activity' (*activité générique*) since it permits the proof of a being that is conscious of its species-being (*essence générique*).

With work and production we have therefore an effective and practical doubling of the agent that is consistent with the engendering of an exterior objective reality, and not a doubling of the self that is only internal to the subject. This is the important difference with respect to idealist theories of consciousness, a difference that Marx does not fail to stress in the *1844 Manuscripts*: 'The object of labour is therefore the objectification of the species life of man: for man reproduces himself not only intellectually, in his consciousness, but actively and actually, and he can therefore contemplate

---

prepares the becoming of labour from within production itself. While considering the becoming-production of natural productivity (that is to say, productivity as the voluntary and conscious engendering of products), and then the becoming-labour of production itself (that is, production as expenditure of subjective labour power), as processes that are both natural and historical and in themselves necessary, Marx places himself in the perspective of a reversal of this double process, more exactly of a surpassing (*Aufhebung*) of work in production and of production itself in productivity, an overcoming by which humans would, in their participation in natural productivity, experience the affirmation of their own power in the form of what he calls their self-activation. These are points to which we will return later, notably in our Conclusion.

[31] Marx, *Early Writings*, 329.

himself in a world he himself has created.'[32] The doubling of the agent in and through its productive activity is what permits it to reveal itself as a conscious agent, but insofar as it is an agent conscious of its species and not merely conscious of itself, in the sense of a singular consciousness of self as a singular subject. Marx elaborates here a concept of consciousness radically opposed to the idealist conceptions that one finds in Fichte or in Hegel's *Phenomenology of Spirit*, and we should not underestimate the importance of Marx's gesture in terms of it being nothing less than a radical critique of the modern philosophy of consciousness insofar as the latter has been, at least since Descartes, taken up with the figure of the philosophy of the subject. The production of objects, the practical elaboration of the objective world, is a doubling which makes manifest in the eyes of the agent its own generic being insofar as it is an objectively generic being, a reality that is just as objective as the products generated by its generic activity. The conception of consciousness that Marx elaborates here is a counterpoint to the idealist thesis that one finds in Kant, Fichte or Hegel (and that returns in Husserl) according to which all consciousness of an object presupposes the consciousness of the self. Marx posits to the contrary that all consciousness is first the consciousness of an object and that it only becomes a consciousness of the self in a secondary and derivative manner, in what is also an essentially pathological process which is none other than that of alienation. Consciousness, according to Marx, is first of all neither the knowledge of a singular self nor the attestation of a subject in opposition to an object; on the contrary, consciousness is originally the knowledge of an essence that is universal and generic, and at the same time the knowledge of a being that takes itself as its own objective reality. Humanity, writes Marx, 'creates and establishes only objects because it is established by objects, because it is fundamentally nature. In the act of establishing it therefore does not descend from its "pure activity" to the creation of objects; on the contrary, its objective product simply confirms its objective activity, its activity as the activity of an objective, natural being'.[33] Through the specific trait of consciousness humanity does not escape nature or the general order of nature: on the contrary, consciousness is humanity's objective and natural knowledge of its own being. By its generic activity, that is to say in producing exterior objects and developing the external objective world, humanity forms at the same time the knowledge of its generic essence as the essence of a being that is itself objective, produced and begotten in the world like any other object.

[32] Ibid.
[33] Ibid., 389.

Far from freeing itself from nature, humanity, through its productive activity that is itself natural, obtains and forms the knowledge of its own existence as a being that is objective and natural. The knowledge that human beings originally form of themselves is therefore a knowledge of themselves not as an exception to nature, but as 'a part of nature',[34] as a 'being of nature';[35] they do not know themselves as subjects or as a self, but as objects among objects, as an objective natural reality in the midst of objective natural reality. 'Man is equated with self', writes Marx. 'But', he adds, 'the self is only abstractly conceived man, man produced by abstraction'.[36]

We will return to this later, but it is at least necessary to remark that there is in Marx's text a radical critique of the modern philosophy of subjectivity as it found its fulfilment in Hegel. In positing that human beings are beings in nature, objective realities at the heart of objective reality, Marx intends to recuse himself from the philosophical and metaphysical gesture that – since Descartes, but with the notable exception of Spinoza – begins by positing that (in Marx's words) 'the essence of man equals self-consciousness'.[37] Positing that the consciousness of self is the essence of humanity, and therefore that the essence of humanity is self or subject, is to posit that any relation to objectivity is an alienated relation, and is therefore to claim that the reappropriation of the self by the self implies the suppression of alienation, that is to say the negation of objectivity: thus the modern philosophy of subjectivity is in some sense led to conclude inevitably that 'man ... is a non-objective, spiritual being',[38] and is therefore an exception to nature, 'a kingdom within a kingdom'. For Marx, however, it is not the relation with objectivity that is in itself alienating; on the contrary it is the conception of the self as a subject that is the mark of substantial alienation, when human beings see their essence reduced to their individual and singular existence, cut off from everything in relation to the objectivity of things, of others as well as of themselves. For generic or species-beings such as humanity, that is to say for beings in which a knowledge of natural objectivity takes form, what is alienating is not the relation to objectivity, but on the contrary the exclusion from it, being deprived of a natural relation to those essential objects which are, for humanity, the things of nature and other human beings. 'Consciousness', states *The German Ideology*, 'can never be anything

[34] Ibid., 329.
[35] Ibid., 389.
[36] Ibid., 387.
[37] Ibid.
[38] Ibid.

else than conscious existence',[39] that is to say, 'that being known' (*das bewusste Sein*): consciousness is nothing apart from being. It is notably not the property of that which is opposed to the totality of objective reality in the positing of a subject; it is on the contrary the natural being really and objectively existing and knowing itself as a being, humanity, which is itself natural and objective, grasping the objective essence of all reality and knowing itself to be no exception to the general regime of natural objectivity.[40] Human beings are not first beings that are conscious of themselves, subjects to which the natural and objective nature of existence would be added as the exterior; according to Marx, as for Spinoza, the opposite must be the case: 'self-consciousness is . . . a quality of human nature . . . human nature is not a quality of self-consciousness'.[41]

It is therefore clear that the vital and natural activity of humanity is specific, and that it introduces into nature an element of novelty relative to the vital activity deployed by other living things. The fundamentally new element introduced by the properly human vital activity is the extension of this activity to all of nature. This extension is inseparably linked to the fact that with humanity the knowledge of natural objective being is formed and appears: this knowledge, insofar as it is knowledge of the essence of objective and natural being, implies taking a perspective on the totality of objective being and therefore on nature in its entirety. The fact that, in taking this theoretical perspective, the knowledge of human beings extends over the essence of nature is indissociable from the practical extension of their vital and practical activity over all of nature. From the productive activity of humanity, insofar as it is productive of objects, emerges the theoretical knowledge of the essence of the same objectivity, and the consequence of this knowledge is the practical extension of this productive activity to all of objectivity. Therefore, where other species are assigned to a single form

---

[39] Marx and Engels, *The German Ideology*, 47.
[40] We are not able to follow Henry in the commentary he has offered on these passages in the *1844 Manuscripts*, leading to the idea that 'man is the product of his own labour . . . on the basis of the same process of self-objectification' (Henry, *Marx: A Philosophy of Human Reality*, 58). Henry attributes to Marx a thesis that is Hegelian and, in a general manner, idealist, according to which all consciousness (of an object) is in truth consciousness of the self. He thereby misrecognises the radicality effected by Marx in which all consciousness is essentially and originally consciousness of an object and only by abstraction consciousness of the self. On this point, Marx's source is certainly not Hegel, but rather Spinoza, who permits him to break with the Hegelian theory of consciousness. We return here to the analysis of Julien Servois in his study 'Etude sur le travail aliéné dans le *Manuscrits de 1844* de Marx', 287.
[41] Marx, *Early Writings*, 387.

of production always involving the same materials and always generating the same products, there is nothing in nature that human work cannot transform and that it cannot appropriate, nothing which humans could not make the material of a production thus far unseen. 'The universality of man manifests itself in practice in that universality which makes the whole of nature his inorganic body.'[42] It is nature in its entirety, and not this or that particular or partial aspect of it, that is the 'laboratory' of human activity; nature is considered in its totality by humanity as a vast arsenal of the means of labour: 'as the earth is his original larder, so too is it his original tool house'.[43] The entirety of nature then becomes for humanity the 'organs of his activity, which he annexes to his own bodily organs'.[44] The terms used in *Capital* are exactly those already used in the *1844 Manuscripts*, where we read that 'Nature is man's *inorganic body*, that is to say nature in so far as it is not the human body.'[45]

At this point it is necessary to ask if it is not precisely this capacity to relate oneself to the entirety of nature, to make it the arsenal of the means of production – a capacity that is as much theoretical (through thought) as practical (through production) – which has as its consequence that humanity leaves nature and is thus affirmed as a historical being. Marx refuses this absolutely, insisting that the specific relation of humanity to the entirety of nature is at the same time the affirmation of the unity of humanity and nature. Thus Feuerbach was right to reaffirm, against idealism, that human beings are a thing of nature, an objective natural reality, but wrong to add that this makes them a simple thing in nature; because the characteristic of this natural being that is humanity is its activity, the particular form of its natural activity. Humanity is a being that 'lives on nature',[46] with this particular characteristic, compared to other living things, that, in one aspect, it knows this, and, in the other, it lives on the entirety of nature considered as the arsenal of the means of production. However, to say that humanity lives from nature is to say that 'nature is his body, with which he must remain in continuous interchange if he is not to die',[47] and this process is such

---

[42] Ibid., 328.
[43] Marx, *Capital, Volume I*, 285.
[44] Ibid.
[45] Marx, *Early Writings*, 328. However, when, in *Capital*, Marx analyses human productive activity and its relation to nature in terms that are similar to the *1844 Manuscripts*, it is with the awareness (absent in the earlier text) that it is an analysis independent 'of any specific social formation' (Marx, *Capital, Volume I*, 283).
[46] Marx, *Early Writings*, 328.
[47] Ibid.

that the relation of humanity to nature is nothing other than the relation of nature to itself through the intermediary or the mediation of humanity. The productive activity of humanity considered as a vital activity is nothing other than the attestation of the unity of man and nature insofar as this is a unified process mediated by humanity: 'that man's physical and spiritual life is linked to nature means simply that nature is linked to itself, for man is a part of nature'.[48] If it is true that nature is unified with itself by the intermediary of human activity as an elaboration of nature, then the inverse is also true: humanity is unified with itself through the intermediary of nature in the sense that human activity reveals and manifests the human essence of nature itself. The defining characteristic of human activity is thus at once to reveal the natural essence of humanity and the human essence of nature. This is only possible because, in objectifying the essential forces of humanity, human activity produces naturally the essence of humanity, and at the same time, inversely, because in elaborating and transforming the natural element humanity humanises nature by its activity.

To which it is necessary to add that this realisation of the naturalisation of humanity and the humanisation of nature both take place in the determinant element that Marx designates when he writes that 'society is therefore the perfected unity in essence of man with nature . . . the realized naturalism of man and the realized humanism of nature'.[49] The active appropriation of nature by humanity and its transformation or productive development are therefore only possible in a social manner; or, as Marx puts it: 'The human essence of nature exists only for social man; for only here does nature exist for him as a bond with other men.'[50] One can see that, contrary to any idea of man as an exception within the general order of nature, Marx posits that through the intermediary of humanity nature does not do anything other than reunite with itself, just as, by its relation to nature, humanity does not do anything other than reunite with itself. Marx now adds that humanity can only relate to itself through the intermediary of nature because its relation to nature is a social relation: it is because humanity is uniquely social that it can relate to nature. For humanity there is no individual relationship to nature: every human relation to nature is a social relationship. This relates directly to the characterisation of humanity as a species-being, a being that is conscious of itself not initially as a self or a singular being, but always as a generic essence of humanity and nature: just as nature, for man, is the essence of

---

[48] Ibid.
[49] Ibid., 349.
[50] Ibid.

nature and therefore the totality of nature or nature as a whole, likewise humanity, for humanity, is the essence or species of humanity, and therefore all of humanity or the totality of humanity as a whole. For human beings, therefore, the 'subject' of the vital human activity of the appropriation and transformation of nature can never be an individual or singular human but must be solely the species of humanity, and therefore all of humanity and a society of humanity – 'subject' here must be placed between quotation marks because, as we have seen, Marx explicitly refuses the idea that a species or society can be considered as a subject.

One can see that Marx is capable of assimilating immediately 'human existence' and 'social existence'; as he writes: 'human existence is social existence'.[51] It is because human existence is naturally social that its existence is generic and that consciousness is itself spontaneously consciousness of the species. Marx is also able to write that '[my] universal consciousness is only the theoretical form of that whose living form is the real community'.[52] My consciousness, one can see, is always first an effect of the 'universal consciousness', that is to say of the consciousness that I possess as the species, and not the consciousness of a singular self, and therefore not a consciousness of 'the self'. But this does not prevent this universal consciousness of the species from being mine, since, according to Marx, there is no difference between the species and the individual: 'the individual is the social being', he writes, adding that 'Man's individual and species life are not two distinct things.'[53] This can be easily grasped, since the human individual is always a socialised individual and therefore a 'social being', in which consciousness can perhaps only be spontaneously a universal consciousness, that is to say a consciousness of the generic. This brings us back to the idea that 'my universal consciousness is only the theoretical shape of that whose living shape is the real community': we can see that to the exact extent that the human vital activity is a necessary social activity, human consciousness is consciousness of the species. As Marx also writes, '[as] species-consciousness man confirms his real social life and merely repeats in thought his actual existence'.[54] In other words, if the generic consciousness takes the inverse form of the singular consciousness of the self, if the consciousness of the species contradicts itself in giving priority to this form of consciousness of the self, it is because actual social existence itself takes the negative and inverted

---

[51] Ibid.
[52] Ibid., 350.
[53] Ibid.
[54] Ibid.

form of a divided social life in which labour has been divided into multiple different tasks, private property has been instituted, and social life has been reduced to relations of competition between individuals. The individual consciousness of a singular self is the contradictory form of a species consciousness inevitably engendered by an 'actual social life' founded on what one could call 'possessive individualism'. This also explains that human consciousness cannot be anything other than the immediate consciousness of a singular self within a form of social existence that abstracts individual existence from society itself. Consciousness can only be singular, can only take the form of consciousness of the self, where actual living social existence is reduced to individual existence, in a negative form of society that isolates and separates rather than uniting and connecting, in which the heart of the social relation takes the negative form of a non-relation, in particular that of a relation of interindividual competition rather than a collective relationship of cooperation and association.

The relation of humanity to nature is therefore the relation of human society to nature. This thesis advanced in the *1844 Manuscripts* would be maintained by Marx in the texts of his maturity such as the *Grundrisse* and *Capital* itself. In the *Manuscripts* it takes the form of an affirmation according to which 'Nature as it comes into being in human history – in the act of creation of human society – is the true nature of man.'[55] It is necessary first to remind ourselves that human history, that is to say the history of human society, is such that a species-being such as humanity can only have a social history. However, the history of human society is also the one and only basis on which it is possible for us to approach nature as such: there is only nature for human beings that have already humanised it, which is to say collectively and socially appropriated and transformed it. For Marx, history means nothing other than this social process of the appropriation and transformation of nature: history cannot be opposed to nature, nor can it be added to it as a qualitatively different strata, as a substantially different order of phenomena, since it is solely through history and as history, insofar as it is history, that there can be for humans anything like a relation with nature. Nature is only a reality for human beings as something social; it has only a historical existence for them. Marx emphasises this when he writes that 'the *social* reality of nature and *human* natural science or the *natural science of man* are identical expressions'.[56] By which it must be understood that for Marx there are only the real sciences of nature, the sciences that take the sensible

[55] Ibid., 355.
[56] Ibid., 356.

world for their object. However, nature is always for us a social nature and thus a nature socially transformed, and the sensible world is always a sensible world humanly produced and socially engendered; it seems then that every science of nature and all knowledge of the sensible world can only be at the same time the science and knowledge of humanity, that is to say, the science and knowledge of the social, and therefore historical, relation of humanity to nature. The natural world is always for humanity the human natural world or the world naturally human, in other words the natural world socially appropriated and transformed and therefore the historical world. 'For socialist man', Marx writes, 'the whole of what is called world history is nothing more than the creation of man through human labour, and the development of nature for man';[57] 'socialist man' here refers simply to those who, like Marx himself, have recognised that the only relation of humanity to nature is social and historical, and who thus admit that 'society is therefore the perfected unity in essence of man with nature'.[58]

One can see that the specific point of view of Marxist philosophy recognises as real and effective neither a natural world existing in itself independent of all relation to human beings and human society, nor a world properly human, social and historical, separated from all relation to nature. What exists is neither a pure nature nor a pure historicity; the error of Feuerbach and of materialism in general is to have posited the existence of the first, while the error of idealism is to have hypostatised historicity as the essential attribute of an imaginary subject conceived as 'spirit'. That which actually exists is the unity of nature and history, and this unity is social. Society is the unity of nature and history: human history can perhaps comprise 'an actual part of the history of nature', only on the condition of comprehending that the human relation to nature is always a social relation and that nature only exists for human beings through the intermediary of the social activity by which it is appropriated and transformed. The only nature that exists for human beings is nature 'which develops in human history', that is, 'nature such as it develops through industry'.[59] However, 'industry' is nothing other than the natural and essential activity of humanity: 'industry as it has developed is the *open* book of the essential powers of man, man's psychology present in tangible form';[60] it is the generic vital activity of humanity, the activity by which humans engender and develop an objec-

[57] Ibid., 357.
[58] Ibid., 349.
[59] Ibid., 355.
[60] Ibid., 354.

tive world in which, because the world is essential to them, they can recognise their proper objective essence. 'The history of industry' is the only real history because it is the process in the course of which human beings exteriorise, manifest, objectify and naturalise their essential forces, while at the same time nature is interiorised, subjectified and humanised. If the only real history is the history of industry insofar as it is the naturalisation of humanity and the humanisation of nature, then one can understand that the unification of nature and humanity, such as takes place in the history of industry, can only be a social unification; if the unity of humanity and nature can only be industrious and can take no other form than the history of industry, then the unity of nature and history, under the only real form that is the history of industry, can only be social. For a species-being such as humanity – that is to say, for a natural being that relates to objects that are essential and vital, such as the things of nature and other human beings which are essential and objective needs – what actually exists is the natural element within which the social and collective process of the appropriation and transformation of the natural world historically unfolds. The 'essential reality', according to Marx, is the unity of man and nature,[61] the historical becoming for and by humanity, that is to say the unity in which 'man has become for man as the being of nature' and 'nature for man as the being of man'; but it is uniquely in and by society that humanity mediates for itself the existence of nature, in the same way that it is only by society that nature mediates for humanity the existence of humanity. The specific nature of humanity is that it is the vital species in which the natural life of the species is accomplished and realised in the historical process that engenders social life. To the thesis of the *1844 Manuscripts* according to which human beings are nothing other than 'nature rendered human'[62] it is necessary to add the sixth of the 'Theses on Feuerbach' according to which 'human essence is the ensemble of social relations':[63] the unity of man and nature is only actual as social life,[64] understood as the totality of historically developing 'practical

---

[61] Ibid., 357.
[62] Ibid., 328.
[63] Ibid., 423.
[64] Nevertheless, according to Marx, this unity of humanity and nature, as the process of the humanisation of nature and the naturalisation of man, cannot be considered in terms of the actual state of things, as a unity accomplished, or a completed process: the unity of man and nature, or the accomplished process of their unification, can only be presented in an authentic state of society, that is to say, by definition, in a state of society that has abolished private property, and, through it, the alienated character of human activity. 'Because it is only in society that nature is for [humanity] a relation

relationships' forged between humans as living beings, that is to say, beings active and passive at the same time, beings who affect each other in and through the very activity they carry out collectively in order to meet their basic and vital needs.

However, if social life or 'the ensemble of social relations' is the necessary form under which the effective reality of the unity of natural life and historical life, it is necessary to note that the preponderance of this unity can be attributed to nature or history: the unity of nature-history can be presented either as a natural power or as the power of history. Put otherwise, N=H can be either $(N=H)^N$ or $(N=H)^H$. This distinction[65] is already introduced by Marx in the *1844 Manuscripts* when he writes that, in the form of social life prior to modern civil society, that is to say in social forms where feudal private property is still the dominant form of property, '[l]abour is . . . not yet grasped in its universal and abstract form, but is still tied to a particular *element of nature as its matter* and is for that reason recognised only in a particular *mode of existence determined by nature*'.[66] In such a social and historical formation, human beings are still more indebted to nature for their products rather than nature itself being a product of their own labour. 'Here the land', Marx writes, 'is still regarded as a part of nature which is independent of man':[67] it is still for human beings prior to and external to their own productive activity, so that this activity still appears to them to be dependent on what is naturally given and inscribed within a natural element which pre-exists and determines it. The unity of man and nature, of nature and history, of nature and of history as a history of social relations of production, is still here predominantly a natural unity, the unity of nature and history is presented under the auspices of nature, or as unity which is itself natural: that is what Marx is saying when he says that the earth is still

> with humanity', that is, under the form of society, in the element of social life in which humanity is reunited with itself by the intermediary of a productive relation with nature. Which is to say that it is by the intermediary of their productive relation with nature that human beings are unified with other human beings, or that there is for the human being a productive relation to nature, necessary for the development of natural and social objectivity. However, the positive form of society and the total affirmation of social life are neither a form nor an actual affirmation. The actual and present moment is characterised by a negative form of society which is in reality a negation of social life insofar as it involves the separation of human beings, their mutual isolation, their reduction to individuality and competition between them.

[65] Alfred Schmidt has emphasised the importance of this in his remarkable and indispensable work *The Concept of Nature in Marx*.
[66] Marx, *Early Writings*, 344.
[67] Ibid.

not recognised as capital, as 'a moment of labour itself'. It is on the contrary human labour that appears as an aspect of the land itself, and therefore as a moment of mediation internal to nature in general. On the other hand, an element of radical novelty is introduced when work on the land becomes 'agricultural labour', when the land becomes capital that only labour is able to valorise: the industrial form of property replaces land ownership, landed property must no longer produce rent but 'wealth', which is only possible once labour is recognised as the exclusive source of wealth. It is now the earth and nature that are moments of industry and of labour, and the unity of nature and history is predominantly historical or affected by the historical, i.e. social, component.

In brief, as Marx reiterates in the 1857 Introduction to *The Contribution to the Critique of Political Economy*: 'in all forms of society there is one specific kind of production which predominates over the rest', and 'in those where capital rules, the social, historically created element [is preponderant]'.[68] It is this that makes it possible to understand that it is uniquely in the conditions that reign under capital, that is to say in modern bourgeois society, that one can form a radically historical consciousness of the world – the consciousness that Löwith, as we have seen, attributed to Marx. The latter, however, having himself enumerated the social and historical conditions of this historical conception of the world, could not be a naive representative of it. The fact that within capitalist society the conditions of production are no longer natural conditions but are the historical results of production itself does not mean that this form of social organisation is freed from any relationship of dependence on nature – despite the ideological consciousness that it has of itself as a purely historical society, the preponderance of historically and socially engendered elements does not suppress the presence of a natural element. Social activity is always the particular modality of an activity that is primarily vital, and historical life has an aspect that is primarily natural. Maintaining this vital and natural foundation against the attempts of abstraction of history and society to place themselves outside of nature and life – this, for Marx, is the nature of a materialist conception of history. If one can say, with Lukács, that 'nature is a societal category'[69] it is nonetheless necessary to add the inverse and say, with Alfred Schmidt, that 'society is a category of nature', in the sense that social forms only ever appropriate and transform a *segment* or a region

---

[68] Marx, *Grundrisse*, 106–7.
[69] Lukács, *History and Class Consciousness*, 234.

'within the still largely unpenetrated total reality, nature'.[70] The reality that actually exists for us (i.e., for humans) can only be a reality consisting of a (necessarily impure) social mélange of nature and history. However, this mélange can itself only carve out a space in the heart of a nature that remains an englobing reality, while not being conceivable as such, as an omni-englobing reality, only from the segment or fragment that we have socially appropriated from it.

This is something that Kosík knew well, as when he notes that 'Man does not live in two different spheres, nor does he inhabit history with one part of his being and nature with his other part. Man is at all times at once in nature and in history.'[71] The historical process by which human beings humanise nature is not capable of reducing nature to being no more than a 'social category' and history. In other words, the subjectivation of the object can never be complete – which does not of course prevent human beings from maintaining the illusion that it can: at a certain stage of the development of their productive forces and in specific social relations (in the present case in capitalist societies, but also in societies of 'real socialism') they can come to truly believe in a possible humanisation and historicisation of nature in the form of its total domination, its complete technical mastery. This, however, is an illusion of power that only serves to conceal, dissimulate and compensate for their lack of power as pure subjects separated from their natural objectivity, compensating for their radical impotence with the delirium of a complete technical mastery of nature, the fantasy of a total domination of nature. Marx never ceased to demonstrate that the historical process is a dual reality: in one part it is the humanisation of nature, but in the other part it is also at the same time the naturalisation of humanity, which is to say the inscription of human beings in nature as a totality that precedes them and on which they depend as part of that totality. This is what Kosík recognises when he writes that, 'as an historical and thus as a social being, [humanity] humanizes nature but also knows it and recognizes it as the absolute totality, as the self-sufficient causa sui, as a precondition and prerequisite of humanization'.[72] The process by which humans practically come to dominate more and more of the forces of nature at the same time as they theoretically come to know its laws does not take the form of the self-constitution of humans as Promethean subjects, masters and owners of nature, and the reduction of nature to an object that is known, mastered, calculated and manipulated at

---

[70] Schmidt, *The Concept of Nature in Marx*, 166.
[71] Kosík, *Dialectics of the Concrete*, 151.
[72] Ibid.

THE IDENTITY OF NATURE AND HISTORY 57

the heart of determinant social relationships, the existence of which would be at one and the same time the condition and the effect of the emergence of capitalism. At the centre of these same relations is the reduction of the majority of human beings to a total lack of power, and it is this that justifies the myth of a Promethean human power over all of nature. Against the myth of the autonomy of an extra-natural subjectivity absolutely subordinating objective nature, and the illusions that inevitably accompany this myth, Marx contends that 'knowledge and domination of nature are socially conditioned' and insists on the 'reality of nature as the absolute totality, independent of man's consciousness but also his existence'.[73] He insists, in other words, on the irreducibility of nature understood as 'absolute totality, independent of the consciousness of man, but also his existence'; he therefore adopts a 'cosmological conception' – which Kosík reminds us is also that 'of Heraclitus and of Spinoza' – according to which 'man recognized nature as the absolute and inexhaustible totality to which he forever anew defines his relationship, throughout history'.[74] Which means that a being that is itself a part of nature can only ever have a partial knowledge and mastery of nature, that there is no possible passage from the finite to the infinite. This is fundamentally different from the delirium (which capitalism is founded upon) of unlimited mastery and knowledge, which culminates in the *apeiron* of the (capitalist) form of the indefinite accumulation of riches, or the unlimited valorisation of value.

For Marx as for Spinoza, the question is thus to know if it is possible to cure this delirium of the mastery of the infinite. The cure can consist of nothing other than the restitution to humanity of a knowledge of its essential finitude, of the native impotence that defines where humans are, insofar as they are parts of nature, arriving at the totality from a part of it and only thereby gaining any knowledge or mastery at all. However, to cure this dream of totalisation, it is necessary to go further still and say that totalisation is impossible not only for humans but in itself. Which means that the 'totality' of nature which Marx refers to, when he writes of humans as parts of this totality, is not a unifiable totality: it is a totality as a definitively exclusive ensemble (in the sense that there is nothing outside of it), but one that is unlimited or 'inexhaustible', to use Kosík's term. Once more, in the terms used by Deleuze in relation to Epicurus rather than Spinoza: the totality of nature 'is not collective, but rather distributive', which means that it is 'an

[73] Ibid.
[74] Ibid.

infinite sum ... a sum which does not totalize its own elements'.[75] Marx, following both Epicurus and Spinoza in thinking nature as 'a principle of the production of the diverse', would thus also recognise that such a principle 'makes sense only if it does *not* assemble its own elements into a whole'.[76] This is because nature itself does not totalise but distributes itself indefinitely, which as a consequence makes it impossible for us to pass from the finite to the infinite, to produce the infinite from the finite, to undertake a progression that would be at the same time a totalisation.

Such a movement is explicitly refused by Marx, for example in the *1844 Manuscripts*, where, to the one who, going back from generation to generation, ends up asking the question 'who begot the first man and nature as a whole?', Marx responds by suggesting a different question: 'Ask yourself how you arrived at that question. Ask yourself whether your question does not arise from a standpoint to which I cannot reply because it is a perverse one. Ask yourself whether that progression exists as such for rational thought.'[77] In other words, this point of view is effectively absurd and unreasonable because it implies that a being of nature adopts a totalising point of view on nature that nature itself ignores. The issue here is not that it would be impossible for a naturally finite being to arrive at such a totalising point of view (to the contrary, it is perfectly possible, and these days that is exactly the problem!), but that such a point of view is radically inadequate to nature and simply does not make sense (this is its 'absurdity', to use Marx's term). How to effectively portray Marx's point of view without putting it into relation with the view Spinoza expresses in Proposition 28 of Part I of the *Ethics*? 'Every singular thing', Spinoza writes, 'or any thing which is finite and has a determinate existence, can neither exist nor be determined to produce an effect unless it is determined to exist and produce an effect by another cause, which is also finite and has a determinate existence; and again, this cause also can neither exist nor be determined to produce an effect unless it is determined to exist and produce an effect by another, which is also finite and has a determinate existence, and so on, to infinity.'[78] Everything hinges on this 'so on, to infinity': from the finite we can only deduce another finite thing; starting from the finite we can only go on to another finite, without hope of ever being able to reassemble the finite in the figure of the infinite that would be a totality. The enumeration of finite determinations cannot be

---

[75] Deleuze, *The Logic of Sense*, 267.
[76] Ibid., 266.
[77] Marx, *Early Writings*, 357.
[78] Spinoza, *Ethics* I, 28; CWS I, 432.

known to its end without the gesture of an ideal and totalising closure that can only take place at the cost of the formation of the illusion of final causes. This is why, to return to Marx, if the practical relations that intertwine us with other human beings result in a practical mastery and theoretical knowledge of nature, it is never such that from this historically and socially limited part of nature they could ever envision the total domination of nature and posit themselves as masters of such a totality: humans, by their relations, engender 'a socio-human reality that transcends nature' and through history define their 'place in the universe'; but they always do so 'within nature and as a part of it'.[79]

---

[79] Kosík, *Dialectics of the Concrete*, 151.

5

With Respect to Contradiction

Marx positions himself, as we have seen, in the point of view from which human beings are seen as naturally active and productive. As natural beings and therefore as part of nature they are beings that deploy a precise and determined vital activity. Considering human beings as part of nature does not deny them all activity, but on the contrary makes it possible to understand that they can express the activity of the whole because they are part of it. In this sense, there cannot be, for either Marx or Spinoza, a natural being that would not be active. Sharing Spinoza's fully affirmative and positive concept of nature, there exists for Marx no real passivity: what is called passivity is nothing other than a privation of activity, a diminished activity, just as falsity and error can only be for Spinoza a privation of knowledge. Passivity does not actually exist in itself; it exists only relative to those that experience it as they are determined to act by something other than themselves and confer, on that which determines them, the capacity to act on them and through them. This is the case, for example, with the relationship between 'the activity of individuals' and their 'forms' or 'modes of exchange'. The problem is to comprehend how individuals can passively endure the relations they enter into with others, how these relations can be relations of passivity, and thus how they are nothing other than the forms of relation through which they are active.

An initial explication consists in saying that this distinction between the activity of individuals and their modes of exchange does not initially exist in a given historical epoch, but that it eventually appears, signifying each time the end of an epoch and its passage to a new period. In other words, initially the modes of exchange and relations of production always correspond to the productive forces and to the state of their development, the former appearing as natural conditions for the deployment of the latter.

The conditions under which individuals have intercourse with each other, so long as the above-mentioned contradiction is absent, are conditions appertaining to their individuality, in no way external to them; conditions under which these definite individuals, living under definite relationships, can alone produce their material life and what is connected with it, are thus the conditions of their self-activity and are produced by this self-activity.[1]

The conditions in which these human beings enter mutually into relation are thus the conditions of 'their self-activity' and at the same time 'products of their self-activity'.[2] However, one arrives at the point where the forms of exchange or the relations of production, the conditions and products of the human activity, become a hinderance (*Fessel*) and a barrier to the productive activity of human beings. Thus begins a revolutionary period which only comes to an end with the engendering of new forms of exchange, permitting the activity and the development of the self by the self (*Selbstetätigung*) of human beings.[3]

This passage from *The German Ideology* is so well known that we no longer notice the problems it poses. It is possible to ask how it is that a condition (of possibility) can end up becoming a limit or fetter. If one responds that it is due to the same development of the productive forces and human activity, then one explains nothing, because, again, one sees neither why nor how it is that, during a determined period, a condition that permits the development of the productive forces could become, in another specific moment, exactly the opposite, that is, an obstacle to the same development. How can the process of development transform its own conditions of possibility into its own fetters and limitations?

[1] Marx and Engels, *The German Ideology*, 91.
[2] Ibid. We are translating the German *Selbstetätigung* as 'activity of the self', which is always strangely rendered in existing French translations as 'manifestation de soi'. By *Selbstetätigung*, Marx intends a becoming-active of the self by the self – a process which can, in Spinozist terms, be called an increase in the power of acting in the sense of an appropriation of one's proper power that makes it possible for one to be the adequate cause of the effects one produces. On *Selbstetätigung* see our work *L'etre et l'acte*, page 159, note 2.
[3] This analysis would more or less be repeated by Marx in the Preface to the *Contribution to the Critique of Political Economy* of 1859: 'At a certain stage of development, the material productive forces of society come into conflict with the existing relations of production ... From forms of development of the productive forces these relations turn into their fetters. Then begins an era of social revolution.' Marx, *A Contribution to the Critique of Political Economy*, 21.

However, there is yet another important difficulty: while Marx follows Spinoza in accepting that the conditions which are the space of the interchange between human beings, and therefore social relations, are always and primarily passively undergone,[4] the text seems to state the opposite – that the forms of exchange are at first perfectly adequate to the activity of human beings, that they are initially integral to this activity, and that it is only later that they become a fetter and a burden to it. In other words, Marx would seem to present the social relations as being initially 'inorganic', in the precise and technical sense of the term, that is to say, as in continuity with activity of human beings, as corporeal as much as spiritual or mental, insofar as these relations are at the same time conditions and products of this activity; it is then only later that they cease to be inorganic and begin to appear as externally and unjustifiably limiting the deployment of human activity, and therefore as contrary to its development.

In order to surmount these difficulties, it is necessary to be attentive to the precise letter of the text: 'The definite condition under which they produce thus corresponds, as long as the contradiction has not yet appeared, to the reality of their conditioned nature, their one-sided existence, the one-sidedness of which only becomes evident when the contradiction enters on the scene and thus exists solely for those who live later (*für die Späteren*).'[5] Which is to say, perhaps, that individuals, at least initially, believe they act within conditions which correspond to their activity, but they only believe and imagine this from their limited and unilateral point of view. In other words, social relations are always something initially passively endured by individuals, and it is because of their submission to these social relations which remain external (which determine, and, in Spinozist terms, limit their power of acting) that human beings imagine these relations as the inorganic conditions of their activity and as fully adequate to them. It is the same exteriority of these social relations, insofar as it is passively endured, that creates the conditions that permit people, given the privation of their knowledge and consciousness, to imagine that these relations are effectively inorganic, that they correspond to their activity as conditions and products of this activity – which is to say that they are imagined as exactly the opposite of what they are in reality, namely relations endured and not possibly willed or chosen, relations that determine their activity rather than being

---

[4] Marx says this clearly in the Preface already cited: 'In the social production of their existence, men inevitably enter into definite relations, which are independent of their will.' Ibid.

[5] Marx and Engels, *The German Ideology*, 91.

determined by it. Always active under conditions that are endured rather than willed, individuals lead a 'unilateral existence': their being is 'conditioned', their consciousness limited, so that the initial effect of submitting to social relations is a privation of that point of view which would permit them to recognise their 'actual conditioned being', that is to say the unilateral and limited character of their existence.[6]

We cannot absolutely wait for the development of their activity (their productive forces) to lead human beings to recognise the forced and external nature of the conditions that determine the development of their existence. The appearance of the contradiction between the forces and relations of production presupposes the adoption of a point of view *exterior* to the social formation in which these relations reign: this is why the contradiction only appears in the eyes of 'those who arrive later', as Marx writes. The contradiction only appears afterwards and retrospectively for those who are liberated from the limited and unliteral point of view that was necessarily that of the actors in the previous social formation. Those who perceive the limited and conditioned character of an existence determined by the social relations of a previous historical period, however, do not perceive that their own existence is also determined by the social relations they endure in the present: '*Späteren*', those who arrive later can only prove themselves with respect to their predecessors; they cannot and will not be able to see it themselves because they have also submitted to conditions they have endured rather than willed.[7] Marx and Engels could not be more clear in stating that the contradiction between the productive forces and the relations of production is the product of an imaginary conception of things, that it is a partial conception, truncated and mutilated: 'dann erscheint diese Bedingung al eine zufällige Fessel, und dann wird des Bewusstein, dass sie eine Fessel sei, auch der früheren Zeit untergeschoben' ('this condition appears as an accidental fetter, and the consciousness that it is a fetter is imputed to the earlier age as well').[8] The 'condition' referred to is the (unchosen) condition in which human beings find themselves; productive and active within a given historical moment, it is understood that this condition was never wanted by them; they find themselves within it as something imposed on them. Marx tells us that this condition appears as a fetter on or a barrier to human activity 'then'

---

[6] Hence also the fact that 'the imagination', the representation, 'that these determined men make of their actual practice, is transformed into the only determining and active power that dominates and determines the practice of these men'. Ibid., 64.
[7] It is not for nothing that Marx and Engels warn us about the risk of 'sharing for each historical epoch the illusion of this epoch'. Ibid., 63.
[8] Ibid., 91.

(*dann*), that is to say, after the fact, and that it thus appears, and more so, as a 'contingent' fetter. It can only be contingent for those human beings who, in belonging to a later era, consider themselves as freed from this fetter, which, in their eyes, could only be possible if it was not necessary, that is to say was not inherent in the essence of human activity, but was on the contrary purely accidental. Here is the basis of the illusion: there is in reality nothing contingent or accidental in anterior human activity or in the conditions of its development; this activity and its conditions were what they always are, namely necessarily determined by causes and independent of the will of human beings. Only ignorance of causes makes it possible to imagine that conditions could have been other than they were, that human activity was artificially restrained, or restrained in a contingent way, that it is something other than human activity deploying itself under determinant conditions. The imaginary mechanism of 'contradiction' is thus born: human beings consider themselves to be free from a limitation that they project onto a previous epoch, a first illusion which is immediately doubled by another consisting of the 'subtle attribution' of the consciousness of this same hindrance to the men of the earlier era, which is why they have set out to break free. This certainly makes the *Späteren*, the latest to arrive, the inheritors of a resolved contradiction and thus fully justified in what they are. But how can we fail to see Marx and Engels' insistence on guarding against such a procedure, which is just as fundamental, consisting in the assertion that 'the average individual of the later stage was always foisted on to the earlier stage, and the consciousness of a later age on to the individuals of an earlier'.[9]

If we turn to the other text that is practically canonical on the contradiction between the forces and relations of production, namely the Preface to the *Contribution to the Critique of Political Economy*, things are far from being as clear as they might seem on a first reading. Marx himself puts us on guard against such a simplifying reading: 'In studying such transformations [the epochs of social revolution] it is always necessary to distinguish between the material transformation of the economic conditions of production,

---

[9] Ibid. 98. It is remarkable that in *The German Ideology*, in the same place that Marx and Engels write that 'according to our conception, all of the conflicts of history have their origin in the contradiction between the forces of production and modes of exchange' (ibid., 83, translation modified), they also write that this contradiction has 'occurred several times in past history, without, however, endangering its essential basis'. It is a strange philosophy of the negative in which, up to now, negativity has never touched the essential and at the same time has conserved the fundamental! However, it is also in this same place that Marx and Engels say that 'the individuals who started the revolutions had illusions about their own activity' (ibid).

which can be determined with the precision of natural science, and the . . . ideological forms in which men become conscious of this conflict and fight it out.'[10] One way of becoming aware of the conflict is to posit it as a contradiction that appears in a previous epoch between the productive forces and the relations of production, between human activity and its conditions, a contradiction which, after its break up, is resolved by the new relations of production that reign in the next epoch, from which one can retrospectively diagnose the previous contradiction. This manner of becoming conscious of a conflict and of grasping its terms is ideological, and it is ideological in the same way that a newly dominant class or social group legitimates retrospectively the revolutionary action it undertakes in breaking with the previous social relations that have limited its role in becoming the dominant class, and which at the same time legitimate its own current domination in demonstrating that it has emerged from the resolution of the contradiction between human activity in general (which is in fact only its own activity) and the conditions that have unjustly hampered it. It is precisely a type of ideological consciousness in that it transfers the negativity into the past and sees only the positivity of the present: this transfer presupposes an inversion, a reversal of the ideological time of the camera obscura.[11] Not only was the previous epoch not contradictory in itself (the forces of production were positively developed in it as far as possible, which to say that it permitted the conditions in which they developed), neither is the present epoch devoid of any negative character, it being understood that negativity does not consist in a contradiction but in a diminution of the power to act, in a separation of human beings from their own power to act – which is not only not absent from the present period, but is at the present time, according to Marx, grander and more radical than ever.

In suppressing the motor role of 'contradiction' it would seem that one has also removed the means of thinking historical change, and with that the possibility of understanding the passage from one historical period to another. On the contrary, we have given the non-imaginary means of conceiving it, and therefore of comprehending the passage from one epoch to another. In what does a definition of this passage consist? It is a 'material transformation of the conditions of economic production', Marx tells us, adding that this transformation can always be 'determined in a scientifically rigorously manner'. There is no need here for the intervention of some sort of 'contradiction', nor for the mysterious work of negativity: it is sufficient

---

[10] Marx, *A Contribution to the Critique of Political Economy*, 21.
[11] Marx and Engels, *The German Ideology*, 42.

to notice and record in their positivity the transformations intervening in material production, as for example technological and technical innovations, and then to describe their effects on the relations of production. On the basis of a positive study of changes internal to the productive activity of human beings, talk about the internal contradictions of the mode of production appears as what it is: a discourse produced after the fact from a retrospective point of view that is essentially finalist and teleological, artificially introducing into the past a negativity or a negation that can only be brought to light in the full positivity of the present. However, if Marx has retained something from Hegel, it is that the first negation of the negative must always in its own turn be negated, and that this is the 'price' it must pay for its rational comprehension, that is to say for its positivity. The theory of contradiction is only an immediate negation of the negative, so it is neither 'rational' (in Hegelian terms) nor 'true' or 'adequate' (in Spinozist terms). From a Marxist point of view, it reveals not the 'language of real life',[12] but the manner in which an epoch becomes immediately conscious of itself in elements of the dominant ideas which are also always those of the dominant class. Marx also takes care to underline, in the same often-cited Preface to the *Contribution*, that '[j]ust as one does not judge an individual by what he thinks about himself, so one cannot judge such a period of transformation by its consciousness'.[13] However, the motive for the resolution of a contradiction that was present and operative in the preceding epoch is understood in exactly the same way in which the immediate self-consciousness of the previous epoch understood the overcoming its conditions, as a self-consciousness that emerges in the representatives of the class that has a material interest in breaking with the previous conditions.

The adoption of the 'language of real life' presupposes beginning by conceiving of human activity as a natural activity, as the vital activity of a natural being and of human beings themselves as they are part of nature. Starting from here, one can conceive that human activity such as it has been up to the present under current social relations, which it is subjected to rather than having chosen them, is and has been an effect of 'the infinite power of nature' (Spinoza) insofar as that power is expressed in humanity. From this point of view (where one sees that the conception of things *sub specie aeternitatis* is also that which permits a true conception of history), the modes of exchange and the relations of production are always and at each time the

[12] Ibid.
[13] Marx, *A Contribution to the Critique of Political Economy*, 21.

inorganic conditions corresponding perfectly to the state of development of the human forces of production. The contradiction between the relations of production and the forces of production can therefore be imagined historically, and can only appear as such in the perspective of those in a subsequent epoch, whose point of view is in turn limited and one-sided due to the fact that it appears in a social formation that submits them to its social relations. The contradiction inherent to a social formation can only be imagined, and can only be imagined retrospectively, in a later social formation, by those individuals who believe themselves to be more clairvoyant than those who have come before and who were blind to themselves. The contradiction in question therefore only exists as such a partial point of view of human modes, but it does not exist from the point of view of the totality of nature: what is called a 'contradiction' is a limitation of human activity due to relations not chosen by men, imposing themselves on them as a limit which diminishes their power to act by determining a certain state of the development of their productive forces.

Marx thus adopts a point of view which permits him to consider that modes of exchange have always been the inorganic conditions and products of human activity: there cannot be in itself and positively a contradiction between human activity and its conditions; such a contradiction can only exist from a point of view that is partial, one-sided and mutilated (Spinoza would say inadequate), of the sort that imagines its own social formation has resolved the contradiction of the previous social formation, and that, as far as it is concerned, the social formation that appears after is without any such contradiction. Marx asserts at the same time that there has never existed a society that cannot in turn be considered from the point of view of a later society as inhabited by a contradiction, *and* that there is in reality or in itself no contradiction, since any previous society will have been both the space and the product of the necessary development of positive human activity as it manifests the very power of nature. This is why the communist 'consciously treats all naturally evolved premises as the creations of hitherto existing men, strips them of their natural character', and renders 'it impossible that anything should exist independently of individuals'.[14] All of these conditions of the activity of actual human beings are inorganic conditions in that they are the product of other human beings who came before them: there is therefore nothing that must be maintained as exterior to the conditions undergone, or considered as being in contradiction with the very activity of human beings and their development.

[14] Marx and Engels, *The German Ideology*, 90–1.

The communist point of view therefore renders impossible, on the one hand, the retrospective projection of a contradiction in a previous social formation, and on the other hand the illusion that the current social form could be understood as a resolution of such a contradiction. However, it is necessary not be fooled by the sense of this illusion: it does not just reside in imagining that our social formation is the resolution of previous contradictions with which it has broken. More radically, the illusion resides in imagining that a social formation contains in itself contradictions. Since a social formation, and the forms of exchange that characterise it, is always at one and the same time the condition and the product of human activity, in which humans undertake the productive power of nature, a social formation cannot contain a contradiction because it is at one and the same time condition and product.

But then, one might object, the communist point of view seems to be identical to the natural and spontaneous point of view of members of a specific social formation who also believe that their modes of exchange or their relations of production are completely adequate for their activity. We have already argued, however, that in thinking this they are victims of an illusion due to the limited character of their point of view which is itself conditioned by the social relations they endure. What is our concern here is that it is through deprivation and a lack of understanding that they imagine they live in social relationships appropriate to the development of their activity: their conditioning by the social relationships they endure has the effect of limiting their consciousness, preventing them from noticing that these relationships decrease their power to act (which is not the same as contradicting it) instead of increasing it. As a result, human beings discover the limitation of their activity and the power of their acting so to speak retrospectively, in projecting onto a previous historical period limitations which they falsely imagine themselves to be free from. The communist point of view is radically opposed to this unreflective and spontaneous point of view: it begins from the contrary position that the separation of human beings from their activity and power of acting has never been greater than it is now. The idea is firstly that social relations have always been relations of subjection, that they have always been the conditions and products of diminished human activity. To this the communist point of view adds the two following elements: First, a human activity is diminished only from a point of view of the human mode of existence, which is to say that human beings have always developed up to now a full and positive activity, although they were not the cause of it. It is positively the very activity of nature that they have deployed so far, but simply by being traversed by it and without being able to recapture it as their own or to comprehend that this activity is also and at the same time theirs. Second, far from the current social form having resolved previous 'contradictions' – which, moreover, were not in reality contradictions – human beings have never been so radically separated from their power to act as they are now, which means that this activity has never been so heteronomous or determined by others than precisely now. History is nothing other than the growing separation of humanity from its capacity to act: the more human beings have developed and perfected their productive powers, and the more foreign these forces have become, the less they have become their own, to the point of becoming, with bourgeois society, the forces of another, namely capital. There is, however, nothing mysterious about this development: in deploying their productive activity and powers under conditions that are at the outset not chosen by them, it was necessary that these forces become more and more opaque and strange, less and less understood and less and less comprehensible, as these forces accumulated the conditions for their own development. Human productive activity, as vital and essential activity, has definitively taken on the characteristics of the activity of another, of an 'alter-activity', against which Marx proposes the prospect of 'self-activation' as a process of appropriation by human beings of their own productive activity and its conditions.

'Only the proletarians of the present day, who are completely shut off from all self-activity, are in a position to achieve a complete and no longer restricted self-activity, which consists in the appropriation of a totality of productive forces and in the development of a totality of capacities.'[15] But the proletarians are 'able' to do this only to the extent that they become revolutionary: the passage to self-activity consists first of all in the revolutionary becoming of the proletarians themselves; the simple fact of being 'totally excluded from any self-activity' is not sufficient to produce such a passage 'mechanically'. As for the self-activation of the revolutionary proletariat, it consists first of all in the self-revolution of the proletariat themselves, that is to say in a practice on the self that allows them to free themselves from any imaginary conception of themselves (starting with the conception of themselves as 'subjects' or as 'subject'): 'the revolution is necessary, therefore, not only because the ruling class cannot be overthrown in any other way, but also because the class overthrowing it can only in a revolution succeed in ridding itself of all the muck of ages and become fitted to found society anew'.[16] The same passage insists on the fact that 'the production on a mass

[15] Ibid., 96.
[16] Ibid., 60.

scale of communist consciousness' supposes 'the alteration of men on a mass scale': this massive transformation of self, the first manifestation of the 'praxis' of self-activation, precedes and renders possible any transformation of society. If self-activation is practical in the sense of 'praxis', it is nevertheless clear that there is no other place of emergence than production, that is to say the deployment of poietic activity, because it is the capitalist mode of production that produces the 'masses' by dispossessing individuals of the objective conditions of the ownership of their own work and reducing them to the status of subjective owners of an abstract labour power. In other words, while the becoming of a mass, in the sense of its formation, is an objective phenomenon characteristic of the bourgeois mode of production, the revolutionary becoming of the mass is another matter: it testifies to a becoming-active by itself of the mass, consisting in the affirmation by the mass of its own power to act under the form of the process of reappropriating all of its own productive forces. Self-activation is therefore a transformation in the poietic order of production: for the masses it is a process of reappropriating their own vital activity and the objective conditions of that activity, a process that we can rightly describe as a reconquest of human activity against the form of work taken by this activity.[17]

This perspective, however, is not that of an ideal to be realised, any more than for Spinoza the sage is a model to imitate: self-activity, as a new poiesis, constitutes an activity of and for the self and not an activity in and for an other which is capital. It begins here and now as an activity on the self, that is to say through a praxis which is a revolutionary activity consisting in an effective rupture of the relation to the self, others and the world.

---

[17] Balibar, *La Crainte des Masses*, 180.

6
The Secondary Nature of the Consciousness of Self

What is it to be a finite mode or, in Marxist terms, an 'objective being'? To be an objective being is first of all to be dependent upon other objects; it is be in an essential and necessary relation with other objects. Such is the case of a human being who, like all living things, depends on other things that are exterior for the perpetuation of its life. These are the objects that are indispensable to appropriate or produce in order to maintain a life; as such they are, as Marx says, 'essential *objects, indispensable to the exercise and confirmation of his essential powers*'.[1] An objective being is therefore a being that is in an essential and vital relation with other objects: 'to say that man is a corporeal, living, real, sensuous, objective being with natural powers', Marx explains, 'means that he has real, sensuous objects as the objects of his being and of his vital expression, or that he can only express his life in real, sensuous objects'.[2] Being objective or existing naturally means having existential and vital relations to objects outside of oneself. This confirms the properly ontological significance of needs and affects as basic as, for example, hunger, which, says Marx, 'is a natural *need*; it therefore requires a nature and an object outside of itself in order to satisfy and still itself'.[3] This is an admission of dependency where a certain body is found to be in need of another body; it is the admission that what is essential to me is in outside of me. It is because the human being has, as Marx says, 'a nature outside of himself' that it 'is a natural being';[4] a being is an objective being, and therefore is really a being, only from the moment it relates to objects that are essential to it and from the moment it is itself such an essential object for another.

---

[1] Marx, *Early Writings*, 389.
[2] Ibid., 390.
[3] Ibid.
[4] Ibid.

This is the first thing Marx borrows from the first chapter of Feuerbach's *The Essence of Christianity*, according to which '[o]ne knows the man by the object that reflects his being'.[5] But what Marx takes from Feuerbach most of all is the idea that 'consciousness of the object is the self-consciousness of the man'; in other words, it is through the objects which are essential to them that human beings become conscious of themselves, or form a knowledge of the self. It is necessary to note that, with respect to both Feuerbach and Marx, this consciousness or knowledge of the self is not to be confused with a consciousness of *the self*, that is to say, with a self-consciousness of the self as a subject in the sense of an ego. It is therefore not self-consciousness that is primary or is the condition of possibility for any consciousness of an object; quite the contrary, it is in the consciousness of the object, and notably in the consciousness of essential objects, that this self-consciousness is formed that is always initially a consciousness of the species, that is, a consciousness of a generic essence rather than the consciousness of a singular existence. 'The way in which consciousness is', writes Marx, 'and in which something is for it, is knowing. Knowing is its only act.'[6] Being conscious (*bewust sein*) signifies first having knowledge of something; since we know there is only a science of the universal, there is therefore only knowledge of the generic or the consciousness of the species. The reason why the self-consciousness of human beings is originally a consciousness of the species, that is to say a consciousness of their generic essence, is that it is formed and can only be formed in the relations human beings have with objects which appear to them to be essential, or which they discover themselves to be essentially dependent upon. It is therefore in the knowledge of these objects upon which they depend that human beings form the knowledge of themselves and of their own essence. 'Hence something comes to exist for consciousness insofar as it knows that something':[7] it is in knowing what they depend upon essentially, knowing the objective reality by which they are themselves posited, produced and engendered, that human beings arrive at knowledge of themselves.

The proximity with Spinoza here is striking. For the latter, consciousness is first the consciousness of the affections of the body, and through their mediation[8] – since the idea of an affection of our body envelops at one and the same time the nature of our body and the nature of the body which affects

---

[5] Feuerbach, *The Fiery Brook*, 101.
[6] Marx, *Early Writings*, 392.
[7] Ibid.
[8] Spinoza, *Ethics* II, 26; CWS I, 469.

ours[9] – consciousness of the body which affects ours, since 'the order and connection of the ideas is the same as the order and connection of things'.[10] More profoundly, however, Marx and Spinoza share the thesis of the secondary status of the consciousness of the self in relation to the consciousness of the object. In Spinoza this thesis is rooted in the more fundamental thesis according to which 'the human mind does not know the human body':[11] in effect the human mind can only have a confused knowledge of its own body since it is only its inadequate idea; the idea of the body of human beings is only adequate in God, insofar as he is considered to be affected by a great number of other ideas which are the ideas of other bodies that determine the body of a human to be what it is in actuality (to the extent that the human body is composed of a great number of other bodies which are themselves determined in a great number of ways by other bodies).[12] The human mind does not have this knowledge of the great number of causes and of bodies which, in it and outside of it, determine the human body to be affected, and therefore it cannot have adequate knowledge of its own body. This is why the true knowledge of the human body can only be in God insofar as he possesses the knowledge of a great number of other bodies, beginning with those that make up the human body itself. In other words, a human being initially knows its body only by the effects produced in it by other bodies, and since it ignores the causes of these effects, it knows its body only in a confused, partial and mutilated manner. The only way for a human being to know its body passes through the effects that this body, considered this time as a cause, is capable of producing on other bodies. The human being's true knowledge of its body and of other bodies therefore presupposes on its part an activity or a becoming-active, in other words, exactly what Marx calls in the *1844 Manuscripts* a *Betätigung*, an activation.

Leaving that aside for a moment, we will focus here on the transition from the knowledge of the body to the mind's knowledge of the self, from the non-knowledge native to the first to the originary unconsciousness of the second. In effect, the human mind, which is already itself the idea of the body, is again an idea that can only be adequate in God insofar as he is considered to be affected by a very large number of ideas, since 'there is in God an idea, or knowledge, of the human mind, which follows in God in the same way and is related to God in the same way as the idea, or knowledge, of

---

[9] Spinoza, *Ethics* II, 16; *CWS* I, 463.
[10] Spinoza, *Ethics* II, 9 Dem.; *CWS* I, 435.
[11] Spinoza, *Ethics* II, 19 and 19 Dem.; *CWS* I, 466.
[12] Spinoza, *Ethics* II, 2 and 3; *CWS* I, 449.

the human body'.[13] The human mind thus cannot know itself for the same reason that the human being cannot know the human body: if knowledge of the human body presupposes the knowledge of a great number of other bodies, then the knowledge of the idea of a human body – that is to say, the knowledge (or the idea) of this idea that is the human mind – presupposes in turn the knowledge of a great number of other ideas. Therefore just as the human mind does not know its body, except by the intermediary of the effects produced in it by other bodies, in the same way the human mind does not know itself, except through the knowledge of the ideas of the effects produced in it by bodies other than its own. It follows that we must say that all consciousness is originally consciousness of something other than the self: the consciousness or knowledge of the body is originally only the consciousness of the effects produced in it by other bodies and not the true knowledge of the body itself; likewise, knowledge or consciousness of the mind is originally only the consciousness of the effects produced in the mind by minds and ideas other than our own. Far from self-consciousness being originary and foundational, it can only be the horizon of a search and can only be achieved on the condition of a becoming-active consisting in a body which becomes the cause of the effects that unfold in it and a mind which becomes the cause of the ideas which occupy it. At the same time, at the foundation of self-consciousness there is something other than consciousness of the self, namely the confused and mutilated knowledge of the body by the intermediary of affects, and the equally confused and mutilated knowledge of the mind through the reflective knowledge of the ideas of affections from the body. Thus no less for Spinoza than for Marx, self-consciousness is not primary; it is neither the original condition for its own self-awareness nor the basis for knowledge of something other than itself: at the beginning and originally, all consciousness is first the consciousness of object(s) that act on and determine (or what Spinoza calls operating) the form of consciousness without it knowing or comprehending how it is acted upon.

This is why for Marx as for Spinoza there is no possible knowledge for human beings outside of the knowledge of nature: true knowledge or a science of human beings cannot be presented as anything other than a knowledge or science of nature. Hence Marx's perspective on the unification in one science of the science of nature and science of humanity, a systematic unification of which we have only one example, and that is in Spinoza's *Ethics*. For Marx, in fact, it is through the deployment of their 'vital activity' – that is to say their industry, their productive activity of appropriation and trans-

[13] Spinoza, *Ethics* II, 20; CWS I, 467.

formation of nature – that human beings come to understand nature; but it is also through this same process that they come to know themselves, to the extent that, as Marx says, 'the history of industry and the objective existence of industry as it has developed is the open book of the essential powers of man, man's psychology present in tangible form'.[14] This why 'industry' is for human beings 'the real historical relationship to nature':[15] it is real nature because it is the only nature that they know by its causes, and also because it is this knowledge of nature by causes that forms their true knowledge of themselves and of their own natural and generic essence. 'The whole of history', Marx writes, is a preparation for man to become 'the object for sensuous consciousness';[16] it is thus the deployment of their vital activity as 'industry' that is the condition of possibility for human beings to have knowledge of themselves, that is to say, knowledge of their own belonging in nature, their inscription in a natural series of causes and effects. It is also, for Marx, this pursuit of the historical deployment of human industry, which is itself 'a real part of the history of nature', that opens the perspective on the unification and identification of the knowledge of humanity and the knowledge of nature: 'Natural science will in time subsume the science of man just as the science of man will subsume natural science: there will be one science.'[17] There is on this point a direct continuity, without the least 'break', between the *1844 Manuscripts* and *The German Ideology*, where one finds the famous declaration that 'we only know one science, the science of history':[18] the perspective, opened in 1844, on the unification of the science of man with the science of nature is maintained, with the added precision that this unification is accomplished under the form of the 'science of history'. However, the reasons why this unification is accomplished in and by the science of history were already known in 1844: the unity or identity of the essence of nature and the essence of man are manifest in the form of a historical process, the collective appropriation and transformation of nature by humans, so that it is uniquely as history, as historical science, that it is possible to realise the unification of the science of nature and the science of humanity. One can certainly divide history into 'the history of nature and the history of man', but 'these two aspects are not separable', since 'the history of nature and the history of men are dependent on each other so long as men exist'.[19]

[14] Marx, *Early Writings*, 354.
[15] Ibid., 355.
[16] Ibid.
[17] Ibid.
[18] Marx and Engels, *The German Ideology*, 34.
[19] Ibid.

Returning for a moment to the primacy of the consciousness of the object in relation to self-consciousness, this is the essential point that Marx inherits from Feuerbach: Consciousness is in effect for Feuerbach a 'generic function', which signifies certainly that it is a quality that belongs to humanity, but also that it is a function by which human beings have a relation to themselves, that is to say to their own essence. 'Consciousness', Feuerbach writes, 'is given only in the case of a being to whom his species, his mode of being is an object of thought'.[20] This signifies that all consciousness is first and foremost the knowledge of an essence: 'being given consciousness', Feuerbach explains, 'is to be capable of science'; 'science is the consciousness of a species'.[21] This is why making an object of oneself insofar as one is a singular individual must not be confused with being aware of the essence: being an object to oneself insofar as one is a singular existing individual, that is, having a 'sense of the self', has nothing to do with the consciousness by which a being is an object for itself not insofar as it is individual but insofar as it is species.

For Feuerbach and Marx, as for Spinoza, all adequate knowledge and all true science is a science of the general, a knowledge of essence and not the knowledge of a singular existence: one might think that it would be sufficient here for Marx to refer to Aristotle, and that it would be unnecessary to refer to Spinoza as well. But everything depends on the factors that comprise 'essence'; that is to say, the general, or the essence, supposes something common to the knower and known, something common in the sense of a relation of reciprocal *suitability* between the knower and the known. The object that Marx calls 'essential' – because in knowing it the knower forms a true knowledge of itself, that is to say a knowledge of its species – is always an object which possesses something in common with the knower, an object that has an essential and vital relation with the knower. It is here, as in Spinoza, that we find the formation of adequate ideas as 'common notions': if the common notions are necessarily general, this is not because they are ideas commonly shared, but first of all because they do 'not constitute the essence of any singular thing',[22] and because they 'represent the composition of real relations between existing modes or individuals'.[23] At the source of the formation of common notions there is the joy engendered by the fact that one enters into a relation with a body that agrees without ours,

---

[20] Feuerbach, *The Fiery Brook*, 97.
[21] Ibid., 98.
[22] Spinoza, *Ethics* II, 37; CWS I, 474.
[23] Deleuze, *Spinoza: Practical Philosophy*, 57.

this joy being itself an augmentation of the power to act that induces the formation of common notions. The latter do not thus provide knowledge of abstract relations between things, but knowledge of these relations 'as they are necessarily embodied in living beings, with the variable and concrete terms between which they are established'.[24] The objects that Feuerbach and Marx qualify as essential are precisely those with which human beings have a vital and necessary relation, a relation of objective necessity, and it is in their relation with these objects, in their vital connection with them, that human beings form a true knowledge of themselves, a consciousness of themselves in their species, as natural beings that are themselves part of nature. This is why Feuerbach can write that 'the object to which a subject essentially and necessarily relates himself is nothing except the subject's own objective being'.[25]

The consciousness of species is a knowledge of that which is in common between human beings and the natural objects with which they are in an essential and vital relation; but here again, as with Spinoza's common notions, knowing that which is in common is what makes possible a rational comprehension of 'the unity of composition of all of nature'.[26] Human beings' comprehending themselves as objective beings susceptible to being composed and combined with other objective beings in the totality of nature is what, for Spinoza, makes possible the common notions, but it is also what makes possible species consciousness for Feuerbach and Marx. Note that Marx is also more consistent than Feuerbach in breaking with idealistic terminology, which is still utilised by Feuerbach when he expresses things only in terms of subject and object. It is not sufficient to say, as Feuerbach does, that a subject knows its own essence in the objects upon which it essentially depends and with which it is in a vital relation of survival; it is necessary to add that in comprehending this it also ceases to see itself as a subject and grasps its own nature, which is that of existing objectively in the objective totality of nature. The relations of real expediency represented by the common notions are an effect of the relations of composition between finite modes, thus they are relations between things rather than relations between a subject and its objects. If one can certainly already conclude that the subject/object relation is secondary and derivative relative to the reciprocal relation of mutual suitability between a natural object and its essential objects, it remains to be seen how and under what conditions this natural

[24] Ibid.
[25] Feuerbach, *The Fiery Brook*, 100.
[26] Deleuze, *Spinoza: Practical Philosophy*, 57.

and original relation of suitability between beings that are equally natural and objective can take the form of relation between, on the one side, a sovereign and founding subject, and, on the other, an objective reality which it relates to through a project of mastery and domination.

7

Subjectivity and Alienation (or the Impotence of the Subject)

It is in this spirit that one can understand something of the theory of alienation that Marx develops in the *1844 Manuscripts*. Taking the word alienation from Hegel, Marx nevertheless radically changes its sense, because for him it no longer makes sense to say that, for a being conceived as a subject, the relation to objectivity is itself alienating and that this relation can only be overcome through the abolition of the alienating exteriority of objectivity, that is to say, through the 'return of the object into the self'.[1] In order to think in these terms it is necessary to posit, as Hegel does, that 'human nature, man, is equivalent to self-consciousness',[2] that is, to the consciousness of the self or the consciousness of self as a singular subject. But if one begins instead to consider human beings as finite modes – that is, as objective and natural beings whose actual essence consists in the effort they make to persevere in their being[3] – then one perceives that it is not the fact of being in a necessary relation to the exteriority of objective nature that is alienating, but on the contrary the fact of being separated from the vital and necessary relation that such a natural being depends on necessarily and essentially. According to Marx, this necessary relation to an exterior nature is far from being an alienating one; it is on the contrary the relation through which human beings prove themselves to be what they are in truth, that is to say, living beings. 'A being that does not have nature outside of itself', Marx writes, 'is not a natural being and plays no part in the system of nature'.[4] In other words, it simply does not exist. A being which does not know relations of necessary composition with essential objects exterior to it

---

[1] Marx, *Early Writings*, 387.
[2] Ibid.
[3] Spinoza, *Ethics* III, 7; CWS I, 451.
[4] Marx, *Early Writings*, 390.

is not itself an objective being: or, 'a non-objective being is a non-being'.[5] Briefly, for a natural and living being, it is not the fact that it has a relation with nature that is alienating, but the fact that it is a separate being: for an objective being it is alienating not to be in an essential relation to objects, to be removed from or restricted from accessing its essential objects. It is therefore alienating to be reduced to a subject, distinct and separated from objects and from the totality of the objective world: it is this which, for Marx, makes a being reduced to subjectivity, to conceiving of itself as a subject, a mutilated being, and therefore an abstract, which is to say an incomplete, being. Abstraction consists here in the fact of being separated from the totality of natural and objective reality and no longer being able to conceive or understand oneself except in opposition to it. Self-consciousness that is not consciousness of species but consciousness of self, that is, the position of self as subject, is the result of an abstraction: the self, as Marx writes, is only 'man as an abstract egoist, egoism raised to its pure abstraction in thought'.[6] Egoism here does not have a moral sense; it designates the position of the individual as ego, that which can only be in abstracting itself from the objective and necessary relations that it enters into with all the other parts of nature.

In Marx, it is therefore the metaphysical concept of man as subject that becomes the object of a radical critique, a radicality for which one can perhaps find a fitting precedent in Spinoza, and perhaps a more recent example in Heidegger. The very reasons that make the conception of the self as subject an abstraction are also those that make it an illusion: as the abstraction of a consciousness that is a knowledge only of effects and not causes, its illusory character lies in the fact that its knowledge is that of a conclusion without premises. This primary illusion is the foundation of all the others: ignorant of the true causes, consciousness transforms the effects that it is conscious of into causes, inserting them into a teleology of final causes. In taking itself for the first cause, it then falls into the illusion of free will, and finally into a theological illusion in which, in order to compensate for its impotence, it invokes a God in its own image, operating by free decrees and final causes. The critique of this triple illusion is not as explicitly developed in Marx as it is in Spinoza, but in the former we can find a critique of the first abstraction that permits the subject to conceive of itself as an exception to the common and objective order of nature. Marx also adds the connection between the metaphysical conception of the subject and a particular form of social organisation: the knowledge produced by modern civil society is

[5] Ibid.
[6] Ibid., 387.

one in which human beings are in effect the object of a subjection which reduces them to the state of independent subjects, separate from each other, connected by the negative space of competition rather than by positive and rational relations of association and cooperation. To the Spinozist thesis of the illusory and imaginary character of the self as subject Marx adds the thesis of its ideological character, and this is why a Spinozist such as Althusser could add that 'ideology interpellates individuals as subjects'.[7]

If the effects of the conception of the self as a subject (and particularly the different illusions these effects engender) are less developed in Marx than in Spinoza, the causes that produce this conception appear to be most forcibly developed by Marx. We find in Marx a reconstitution of the essentially pathological historical process that leads human beings to conceive of themselves as subjects. The 'pure subjectivity without object' ('without object' in the sense that the relation to an object appears to be secondary to the subject, not essential, not vital, and in every way always first determined by the subject) is the latest historical result of a process that consists in the dissolution of all the natural and vital bonds that make the human being a naturally objective being inscribed within the totality of a naturally objective reality. The major steps in this process are described in the *Grundrisse*, where Marx argues that

> It is not the *unity* of living and active humanity with the natural, inorganic conditions of their metabolic[8] exchange with nature, and hence their appropriation of nature, which requires explanation or is the result of a historic process, but rather the *separation* between these inorganic conditions of human existence and this active existence, a separation which is completely posited only in the relationship of wage labour and capital.[9]

The unity of human beings with nature, with the natural conditions that permit the exchange between themselves and nature, does not need to be explained because it is the situation at the origin, and thus any search for it would be a vain metaphysical quest for origins and beginnings: the situation at the departure (for which it would be vain to demand proof) is that of beings deploying their natural and vital activity of production, their productive forces, in an element of determined and given relations that interweave

---

[7] Althusser, *On the Reproduction of Capitalism*, 261.
[8] *Stoffwechel* can be clearly translated by 'metabolism'.
[9] Marx, *Grundrisse*, 489.

the relations between themselves and the rest of nature of which they are part. On the other hand, what does demand an explanation, and can only be conceived as a long and slow process, is the separation; that is, how the connection between human beings and the deployment of their vital activity was broken (as much as these connections present themselves in the form of relations, as relations between human beings and nature and human beings and themselves).

It must be understood that the unity which precedes this separation is not a natural unity in the sense of a pre-social natural state: such an opposition of the natural and the social makes no sense for Marx (and even less so for Spinoza). But what must be stressed is that this unity certainly exists under socially determined relations, for example under feudal relations. It therefore possesses a historical dimension, but this historical dimension remains subordinated to natural conditions and is dominated by them. It acts then as a 'pre-bourgeois relation of the individual to the objective conditions of labour',[10] a relation characterised by the fact that 'just as the working subject appears naturally as an individual, as natural being – so does the first objective condition of his labour appear as nature, earth, as his inorganic body'.[11] What is important in this analysis of the pre-modern and pre-bourgeois forms of the labour process is that in them human beings do not produce the conditions of their labour, but find them as 'something existing in nature and which they presuppose'.[12] In other words, if, in these conditions, the life of human beings is founded on production, and if the characteristics of this production as human production are always already present – namely that it can only be social – it nonetheless remains the case that it rests on natural conditions, immediately given and simply found, which are determinant of this production, and therefore the unity of human activity and its own conditions (conditions present in the form of the relations of human beings to each other and with nature) remains here a unity under natural domination.

Everything changes, however, with the appearance of the 'bourgeois', which is to say the modern, form of production, in which, from that point onwards, the conditions of production are no longer simply found as a nat-

---

[10] Ibid., 488.

[11] Ibid. It is worth noting the persistence up to the *Grundrisse* of the characterisation (already present in *1844 Manuscripts*) of nature as the 'inorganic body of man'. According to the *Grundrisse*, in pre-bourgeois forms of production, humans comport themselves towards natural conditions of production as 'natural presuppositions of humanity' that are 'the extension of their body' (491).

[12] Ibid., 488. Translation modified.

ural given, but are socially produced: from that point onwards they are themselves the result of production, to the extent that these objective conditions of labour are present under the form of a social and historical relation determined by capital itself. A certain number of conditions are necessary for the appearance of the modern form of production: first of all the 'dissolution of the relation to the earth . . . as natural condition of production',[13] in the sense that human beings cease to be, through the intermediary of the commune and its members, owners of the earth (there must therefore be an expropriation of the majority of humanity and a concentration of land ownership in the hands of a few, in the form of private property). Second, it requires the 'dissolution of the relations in which [the individual worker] appears as proprietor of the instrument [of labour]',[14] and where this possession of the instrument is recognised in virtue of their natural aptitude, 'their particular skills' – which means nothing other than that labour ceases to have value as a 'personal work' linked with the individual who undertakes it. These two primary conditions, once assembled, engender in themselves a third: the 'dissolution . . . of the relations in which the workers themselves, the living labour capacities themselves, still belong directly among the objective conditions of production'.[15] When the worker is a slave or a serf, they are themselves, as a natural or living thing endowed with natural forces, one of the natural and objective conditions of work. This ceases when the objective condition of production is no longer the worker himself, as living worker, or a living working being, but labour considered as a pure labour power. Only capitalism succeeds in this achievement of no longer considering the worker as a living and working individual, but instead treating their labour alone as an objective condition of production: 'For capital, the worker is not a condition of production, only work is.'[16] The connection of work with the living worker is broken, it is no longer a natural condition of production; the worker becomes free labour, which is to say, 'labour power without objectivity, purely subjective'.[17] This force or power to work is no longer a natural force to the extent that it is no longer the capacity of a natural and living objective individual, existing objectively, and there is no longer an object with which it is naturally intertwined and to which it must naturally be applied. As no longer a natural force of a living being but

---

[13] Ibid., 497.
[14] Ibid.
[15] Ibid., 498.
[16] Ibid.
[17] Ibid., 496.

the abstract power of a 'subject' without objective reality, it now only exists socially in being appropriated by another, namely capital. It is the purely social and historical character of labour, rather than its basis in nature, that makes it (as the human capacity of labour in general) an objective condition of production. As a reality no longer natural but entirely social, work becomes exchange value for the free worker, who exchanges his salary for the equivalent value of goods necessary to reproduce his capacity to work; work is no longer use value except for capital itself, which buys labour for money only to increase money – that is to say, to valorise itself.[18]

The process which leads to the reduction of the human being to the status of subject is thus first that of a systematic and progressive dissolution of a certain number of relations: dissolution of the relation to the earth, dissolution of the natural relation of the worker to his or her instrument, and finally dissolution of the natural relation of workers to themselves, along with the integrity of the natural and living characteristics in the objective conditions of production. It is tempting, at least initially, to think that this process of successive dissolutions is itself a process of liberation,[19] to the extent that it progressively dissolves all types of relations that human beings do not will for themselves, all relations that are imposed naturally on them and which they find themselves immediately subject to without ever having chosen them. It would then be the relations that human beings endure as parts of nature that would be gradually dissolved as the bourgeois relation takes hold, as a mode of production characterised by the fact that its conditions are not found but produced and engendered socially. How then is it possible to consider this process as 'pathological', indeed as the greatest alienation ever experienced by human beings? It is because alienation must be understood as the separation of human beings from their capacity to act, and this separation has never been greater than under the modern conditions of production. It is the same dissolution of the natural and immediate objective relations, which human beings had always simply found, that leads to the massive separation of human beings from their proper capacity to act. There is no greater lack of power than that of a human being reduced to a 'purely subjective labour

---

[18] Ibid., 498.

[19] The liberatory character of this process is demonstrated with the appearance of the salaried worker, that is, an individual who disposes freely of their own labour power and is capable of entering into a contractual relation with the user of that labour power. However, this 'liberty' of the salaried worker is an essential condition of a particularly capitalist exploitation, notably because with the 'free worker' surplus labour is extorted without the open constraint and violence characteristic of ancient slavery and feudal servitude. Marx, *Capital, Volume I*, 346.

power' and 'without objectivity' after the dissolution of its immediate relations with the natural and objective conditions of its capacity to act, that is to say, the development of its vital and productive activity.

Human beings are reduced to the impotence of pure subjectivity at the same time that their labour is reduced to a mere 'expenditure of human labour power in the physiological sense'.[20] 'Before'[21] this reduction, human beings are first of all and essentially natural and living individuals who are naturally constrained, by virtue of 'an eternal natural necessity',[22] to be living and productive beings. It is nature itself that constrains them to produce and engender objects that are use values insofar as they permit human beings to satisfy essential and vital needs. These use values are themselves evidence of the appearance of human beings in nature, as part of it, to the extent that these use values are products of a modification of the form (or a transformation) of natural materials by labour, which is to say by the application of 'natural forces'. The production of use values appears in this context as the effect of a collaboration between human labour, as a sort of useful labour, and nature itself: 'Labour is therefore not the only source of material wealth, of the use values it produces . . . labour is the father of material wealth, the earth is its mother.'[23] Marx states this again in 1875 in the 'Critique of the Gotha Program': 'Labour is *not the source* of all wealth. *Nature* is just as much the source of use values . . . as labour, which itself is only the manifestation of a force of nature.'[24] With the dissolution of the different relations previously enumerated, it is also this *collaboration* (in the literal sense of the word) between human beings and nature that is interrupted, or at the very least ceases to be visible and apparent: the 'useful labour' that is imposed on humanity by virtue of 'eternal natural necessity'[25] is no longer the primary form taken by human work. Labour now refers to exchange value or the commodity itself as value, and is no longer the vital

---

[20] Ibid., 137.
[21] It is necessary to use quotation marks here because this 'before' does not relate to a past era for which Marx would nourish a form of nostalgia. 'Before' does not have a temporal sense to the extent that human beings have never ceased to be and can never cease to be 'parts of nature': it is simply that the meaning of their existence (as the co-implication of the being of humans and the being of nature) is now obscured, or rather forgotten, and the comprehension that human beings have of themselves in their existence as subjects is nothing other than the form of this forgetting.
[22] Ibid., 133.
[23] Ibid., 134.
[24] Marx, 'Critique of the Gotha Program', 341.
[25] Marx, *Capital, Volume I*, 133.

and active power of a naturally working individual transforming a given material into a useful form for the satisfaction of vital needs: labour is on the contrary dissociated from its connection to a working and living individual and becomes a human capacity of labour in general, reduced to a general and anonymously quantifiable power that is therefore expressible by the general equivalent that is money.

As long as the use value of the commodity prevails, the quality of labour as useful and living work – as a formative activity of use value – is decisive, and this quality of work involves both the qualities of the working individual and the qualities specific to the objective conditions of work (in particular the qualities of the material worked on and of the labour undertaken): work is then itself a 'particular use value',[26] that is to say, a 'value for use' qualitatively distinct from the value of use of other work, of work provided either by another individual or under different conditions. But from the moment exchange value reigns, labour is no longer a particular 'use value' but a 'value for the use of value'.[27] One then enters into a relation of labour/capital in the extent to which labour is no longer useful because it satisfies a need, the creation of richness, but because it creates value, that is to say, increases the objectified value against which it is exchanged. The capitalist does not exchange with the worker a certain quantity of accumulated labour or objectivity against his or her living labour because of a need for the labour of the worker, in the sense that their labour represents for them a use value, but because capital needs to add to the value of its objectified labour: living labour is from that point forward only useful for increasing the value of objectified labour.

This means that the qualitative dimension of living labour as useful labour is neutralised, and labour increasingly becomes a quantifiable magnitude. Useful labour, which is formative of use values, is always a qualitative labour, directly connected to the qualities put to work by the individual who works. In contrast, labour as the general human capacity to work is without qualities and is therefore quantifiable: it is the anonymous and general activity of human beings without qualities that are precisely its 'subjects'. The subject is considered here as the largest abstraction, as the simple support of an abstract capacity to labour susceptible to being actualised as such in whatever concrete labour. Two labours that are themselves distinct, such as tailoring and weaving, are only considered as 'two different forms of the

---

[26] Marx, *Grundrisse*, 466.
[27] Ibid.

expenditure of human labour power':[28] what is retained is only what these two different productive activities, in themselves qualitatively distinct, have in common, namely that 'are each a productive expenditure of human brains, nerves, and muscles, and in this sense are human labour'.[29] This systematic disqualification of all labour – the reduction of all productive activity to what it has in common, namely a certain quantifiable expression of human labour power – cannot be done without human beings themselves being reduced to the state of a simple subjective support for this same force or labour power; this is why in *Capital* Marx notes that 'in civil society . . . man as such plays a very mean part'.[30] In fact, the only role he plays is that of the 'average man', in the sense of the man who embodies the mean, the proprietary subject of labour power which owes nothing to its own qualities capable of being implemented by the individual. Considered as proprietary subjects of labour power, all individuals are identical: 'each of these units is the same as any other, to the extent that it has the character of a socially average unit of labour power and acts as such'.[31] The labour power that the subject possesses is determined *a priori* and known in advance, independently of the qualities of the individual considered in their singularity as a living and working individual: this labour power is determined as a function of the 'labour time which is necessary on average' for the production of commodities; and this average necessary labour time is itself determined by 'the conditions of production normal for any given society and with the average degree of skill and intensity of labour prevalent in that society'.[32] This is why a change in the means of production, such as the introduction of power looms, effects a reduction of the socially average labour time necessary for the production of the same commodity, suddenly devalorising the labour power, and reducing the only good possessed by human beings to the abstraction of pure subjectivity.

[28] Marx, *Capital*, Volume I, 134.
[29] Ibid.
[30] Ibid., 135.
[31] Ibid., 129.
[32] Ibid., 120. Labour as the human power to work in general, as socially necessary on average labour time, is what could be called, from a Heideggerian point of view, the labour of the 'they'. To the Heideggerian thesis according to which the subject of modern metaphysics is a figure of the 'they', Marx makes it possible to add that the 'they' is not the subject of 'production' in general, but precisely the subject considered as the owner of labour power in general. There exists in effect, according to Marx, an 'authentic' concept of production which is not entirely absorbed by production conceived as the consumption of the power of labour in general. We will return to this in the conclusion.

The reduction of human beings, by this abstraction, from natural and living beings to the state of 'subjects' as owners of a socially average labour power indicates at the same time the completion of their reduction to a radical state of impotence: for the individual to be conceived and to conceive of itself as a subject it is necessary that it see itself withdrawn and subtracted from the objective conditions of its natural activity; in other words, it is necessary that 'the real conditions of living labour' (the material worked on, the instruments of labour and the means of subsistence which 'fan the flames of the power of living labour') become 'autonomous and alien existences'.[33] 'The greater the extent to which labour objectifies itself', Marx writes, 'the greater becomes the objective world of values, which stands opposite it as alien – alien property.'[34] Reduced to the condition of being the support for an abstract and subjective labour power, the living and working individual sees these objective conditions of its effective and living labour escape it and become autonomous as the object of another subject: the objective conditions of labour are no longer the essential and vital object (*Gegenstand*) of a being equally objective (*gegenständlich*) which is the living and working individual; they are on the contrary the substrates of a vital and essential object that has become an object for another.[35] However, this other appears in turn as a simple property of these same objective conditions of labour. It takes the figure of a subject and is not itself in an essential and vital relation with the objective conditions that it appropriates: it relates to them as a subject to its predicates, as a substance to its attributes. The objective condi-

---

[33] Marx, *Grundrisse*, 454.
[34] Ibid., 455.
[35] We find here the analyses proposed by Marx and Engels in *The German Ideology*, analyses that are developed further in the *Grundrisse* and in the first volume of *Capital*, but not without being substantially modified and even challenged. To return to the diagnostic of *The German Ideology*: 'the productive forces appear as a world for themselves, quite independent of and divorced from the individuals, alongside the individuals' (*The German Ideology*, 95). The productive forces, which exist only 'in the commerce and interdependence of individuals', are detached from the individuals, becoming an objective life detached from the active commerce between them. Already in *The German Ideology*, this detachment of the productive forces from the living and vital exchange between individuals is nothing other than the transformation of these individuals into simple subjective supports, abstract and impotent with respect to these same forces (to the point that they are only the private owners of a force of production abstractly interiorised and subjectified in them): 'we have a totality of productive forces, which have, as it were, taken on a material form and are for the individuals themselves no longer the forces of the individuals but of private property, and *hence of the individuals only insofar as they are owners of private property themselves*' (95).

tions of living labour are thus 'the wealth of an alien subject, indifferent and autonomous from the labour power';[36] this 'alien subject' is nothing other than capital, for which labour, reduced to labour power, is nothing other than the condition of its own self-valorisation, use value for value.

This is why the living worker, already dispossessed of its objectivity (*Gegenständlichkiet*) and reduced to 'the solely subjective existence of labour power', not only the reduction of the objective conditions of labour to an object (*Objekt*) of another subject, but the worker becomes an object to another subject, the attribute of an alien substance. The process is thus one in which an objective being (*gegenständlich*) – the natural and living individual – loses its living relation to its own essential objectives, is reduced to a pure object without essential object (*Gegenstand*), and becomes itself an object of another subject – not in the sense of an essential object but more in terms of a predicate or the attribute of a substance. The expenditure of labour power is used to valorise the objective conditions of labour which are the property of another: labour thus appears, in Marx's terms, as 'the accessory' of these objective conditions, which appear as the counterpart, as 'substance'.[37] Here is the grand reversal: the objective conditions of labour are no longer the conditions of the realisation of living labour; on the contrary it is labour, considered as the simple expenditure of an abstract and subjective power, that becomes itself the condition of the valorisation of the objective conditions of labour which are themselves that of labour objectified and accumulated.

Two pure subjects are from that point onwards brought face to face: *on the one side*, the subject as the owner of an abstract capacity of labour; *on the other side*, the subject as the owner of the objective conditions of the expenditure of this power, that is to say, as capital which appears 'as a subject exercising domination'.[38] In place of individuals interacting with one another and with essential objects as they are found, appropriated and produced, we have from this point forward subjects, as simple neutral supports for an abstract potential to work, in relation with the grand macro-subject of capital that exchanges objectified labour for the expenditure of subjective labour power to be used for its own valorisation. We therefore have, on the one side, an intersubjective relation, and on the other a relation between abstract terms (namely the supports of the human capacity for labour power in general). The relation of these abstract terms with the capital subject are like the

---

[36] Marx, *Grundrisse*, 455. Translation modified.
[37] Ibid.
[38] Ibid., 465. Translation modified.

relation of a substance to its predicates – and these intersubjective relationships come to replace the interindividual and social relations which are the natural relations between objective beings that individualise themselves in the vital milieu of a natural activity of production. In the *Grundrisse*, Marx continues his examination of the nature of the social relation or the relation of production, which in capitalism takes the privileged form of an intersubjective relation: 'the worker produces himself as labour capacity, as well as the capital confronting him, while at the same time the capitalist produces himself as capital as well as the living labour capacity confronting him. Each reproduces itself by reproducing its other, its negation.'[39] The worker conceives of himself not as an objectively living individual or part of nature, but as a subject, which is to say as a labour power that is purely subjective and without an object; it becomes inevitable that it will always already have instituted and recognised (in the Hegelian sense of the word) capital as the subject facing it. Two subjects are found in a relation in which each can only be in relation to the other: the relation to the other is essential to the affirmation of each, although at the same time each negates the other in affirming itself. Each finds in the negation that the other makes it undergo the paradoxical condition of its affirmation: if something happens in Marx to the Hegelian analysis of the relation of master and slave, it certainly happens here, in this intersubjective relationship, where the need to exist is at the same time the need to be negated by the other, only this is now seen as a perfectly pathological relationship. It is necessary for Marx to escape such an intersubjective conception of social relations, which can only be done by starting from production and demonstrating how social relations are immanently structured by the vital and natural activity of production.

In place of social relations between natural beings that are individualised in these relations – insofar as these relations are also the form of the deployment of a natural and transindividual force of production – we have subjects, considered as already constituted, that enter into relationships with each other only under the form of an abstract quantitative compulsion that leads to the production of a mass; that is to say, individuals are 'transformed ... into free workers', freed 'from the objective conditions of work'.[40] The infinite qualitative diversity of individuals who have a living and objective relation, at once to each other and to the objective conditions of their activity, is extinguished in the mass production of abstract subjects as identical supports of the same labour power. The process that reduces human

---

[39] Ibid., 458.
[40] Ibid., 503.

individuals (or modes) to pure subjectivity, which makes them all equally and identically subjects, is also the process that engenders the anonymous mass of interchangeable subjects: the metaphysical 'subject' therefore exists actually and concretely in the form of the 'they' of an anonymous mass of human beings without quality,[41] in the form of individuals living as if they were 'bird free' (*vogelfrie*) – that is to say, as subjectivities transformed into subjects by the subject of capital which is their other.

---

[41] 'Without quality' in the sense of a quality proper to each singularly, because on the contrary they have the quality in common of being abstractly universal depositories and owners of labour power.

8

The Factory of Subjectivity

It is necessary to insist here on the remarkable continuity of Marx's analysis in the works that followed the *1844 Manuscripts*, not just up to the *Grundrisse* but including *Capital*, beyond the differences of vocabulary and form which are themselves comparable to the different 'ways' in which one can try to find the right way to express something. The *1844 Manuscripts* present the situation of the worker as that of a being 'without object' (*gegenstandlos*): in other words, if the worker, like every living being, is essentially an objective being, a being that has vital relations to objects that are essential (objects that are the objective conditions of its proper activity), then the situation of the worker as a being without object, and therefore as a non-objective being, an unnatural (or denatured) being, is one a sense of loss which is in fact that of alienation. It is the theme of reversal – from an objective being to a non-objective being – which is mobilised to make sense of this state of alienation. The object of this reversal is work considered as 'productive life', as 'vital activity'. The reversal is thus only comprehensible from the place of the natural form of labour as a vitally productive activity. The natural situation is one in which 'the worker can create nothing without nature, without the sensuous external world'.[1] The natural condition[2] is characterised

---

[1] Marx, *Early Writings*, 325.
[2] This natural situation is not a 'primordial condition', a concept that Marx rightfully criticises in the same pages: 'We must avoid repeating the mistake of the political economist, who bases his explanations on some imaginary primordial condition. Such a primordial condition explains nothing. It simply pushes the question into the grey and nebulous distance' (ibid., 323). It is not a matter of Marx giving the natural situation of labour the status of an original situation, in the same way that 'theology explains the origin of evil by the fall of man, i.e. it assumes as a fact in the form of history what it should explain' (ibid). The natural situation of labour – insofar as it is defined in terms of the continuity between the individual as living labour and the

by a relation of perfect continuity between the worker (as a natural being whose natural activity is productive activity), their work and nature: work is here the vital activity of a natural and objective being existing as part of the objective totality of nature. It is this situation that underlies the idea, expressed by Marx a few pages later, according to which 'nature is man's inorganic body.[3]

What Marx refers to in this passage as the 'stage of the economy' (that is to say, modern civil society, or what he will later refer to as the capitalist mode of production) is marked by the historical accomplishment of the rupture of the continuity between a living and working being, its vital activity (work or production), its vital milieu (where it finds the objective conditions of its activity), and the products of this activity. How does the current situation look as the completion of this historical process of negation of the natural situation?

> The more the worker appropriates the external world, sensuous nature, through his labour, the more he deprives himself of the means of subsistence in two respects: firstly, the sensuous external world becomes less and less an object belonging to his labour, a means of life of his labour; and secondly, it becomes less and less a means of subsistence in the immediate sense, a means for the physical subsistence of the worker.[4]

What we find definitely undone here is the essential connection between work and its object: the sensible world or exterior nature is essentially the object of work in that it is the means of subsistence of labour, that which work nourishes itself upon. The actual situation is such that the more the worker works the less they work on the object, in the double sense that, first, the conditions of labour (the matter worked on, the tools of labour) appear less and less as a part of labour and more and more external to it, and, second, the product of labour is increasingly exterior to labour. At the same time, given the external nature of work that is less and less immediately a means

> objective conditions of its activity and product – is not conceived by philosophy as a historical fact since the facts of history are those of the reversal of this natural situation: the natural situation expresses the essence of productive activity, the essence of the relation of this activity to its proper conditions (it being understood that the historical fact – that is to say, the very fact of history – is the negation of this essence, in the sense that the historical conditions, as historical, have so far never allowed the affirmation and existence in the action of this essence).

[3] Ibid., 328.
[4] Ibid., 325. Translation modified.

of subsistence, it must be undertaken more and more in order to be a means of subsistence for the worker, but the more it is undertaken, the less it is a means of subsistence in terms of the initial logic of the increasing exteriority between the worker and their object. It is thus the very essence of work that is denied, in the sense that it is prevented from asserting itself in the very activity of the worker. The essence of labour is in effect that it 'cannot live without objects on which to exercise itself';[5] but labour is now constrained in the current situation of 'living without an object'. If the essence of labour is the vital productive activity of human beings insofar as they are natural, then it is necessary to say that the historical realisation of this essence, in as much as it has been accomplished in the current situation, has consisted of nothing other than its very negation: history has completed nothing other than the total denaturalisation of vital productive activity, arriving finally at the reign of a radically disobjectified labour.

The fundamental characteristic of labour is now therefore the 'loss of object': the work is without object and the worker is a non-objective being. This is demonstrated by the fact that the worker no longer constitutes him or herself by virtue of their activity in relation to their own object of labour: far from having an essential relation to the object of their labour as an inorganic body, the worker, from now on, is a worker 'in that he receives an object of labour, i.e. he receives work'.[6] Which means that productive activity is nothing more than a pure subjective power which, in order to be actualised and deployed, must wait for the exterior objective conditions to be provided for it, conditions without which this power is nothing. We find in this situation, which is itself absurd, that a living being whose work is a naturally vital activity must now wait to *receive* work that it is *given* to it when it is given the means of work in the form of the material to work on, the tools of work, and the means of subsistence which have as their characteristic that they are the property of another, namely of capital, in other words, work accumulated and objectified. Far from being what it is essentially – namely the expression, the deployment in action and the positive affirmation of the essential vital forces of a living being – work is no more than the purely negative process of the impoverishment of the worker, that is, his reduction to the state of being the subjective support for a pure capacity for work which must wait for a number of conditions to be supplied from the outside in order to manifest itself.

We see this idea reprised in *The German Ideology* and then in the *Grundrisse*, according to which the production of subjectivity is at one and

[5] Ibid.
[6] Ibid.

the same time the negative process of impoverishment, of progressive destitution, and a reduction to impotence resulting from the rupture of the essential relation of a living and naturally active being to the essential objects of its activity.[7] At the same time, the living and working individual is through its own labour dispossessed of the objects of its labour, attributing to itself only a perfectly abstract quality having only a nominal existence, that of being 'a worker' – a purely internal and subjective quality without a real relation to any object. It is thanks to this inherent quality that the subject hopes to live: 'The culmination of this slavery is that it is only as a worker that he can maintain himself as a physical subject and only as a physical subject that he is a worker.'[8] The worker is a physical subject in the sense that the really existing living individual can only continue to live if they maintain their quality of being a worker by virtue of their purely abstract ability as a worker, a subjective capacity which the subject is recognised as being a depositary of. Reduced thus to the state of being the subject of an abstract capacity to work, the individual is at the same time dispossessed of any mastery of the conditions that would maintain its own life: the worker's capacities now depend on objective conditions (an object of labour, tools of labour) that they are not able to procure by themselves, and which must be furnished from the outside by another. It is certainly the subject possessing an abstract power of work, a pure labour force, which appears here in Marx's text, in the form of a perfectly helpless subject, definitively dispossessed of any mastery of the effective conditions for the perpetuation of its own life.

The concept of labour power that one finds in *Capital* does not contradict this analysis: 'Labour-power', Marx explains, encompasses 'the aggregate of those mental and physical capabilities existing in the physical form, the living personality of a human being, capabilities which he sets in motion whenever he produces a use-value of any kind'.[9] As such, taken together, these physical and intellectual qualities constituting 'labour power' are considered as pure capacities that exist simply to be put to work in the conditions of production in order to have any use value. These qualities of a 'living personality' only exist as pure capacities, considered as things possessing a use value once they are sold, or, more precisely, as only having a use value when they are sold for a specific duration. Marx's insistence on the destitution of the worker reduced to selling the use of qualities that exist in him or her only as a potential is certainly less explicit in *Capital* than in the

---

[7] 'What is life', asks Marx, 'but activity?' Ibid., 327.
[8] Ibid., 325.
[9] Marx, *Capital, Volume I*, 270.

1844 Manuscripts or the *Grundrisse*, but 'the owner of their labour power' is nevertheless described as the completion of the reduction to the bare minimum of 'the living personality' of the worker. What conditions must be in place for the possessor of labour power to sell it as a commodity and for the possessor of money to be able to buy it? The essential condition is that 'the possessor of labour power, instead of being able to sell commodities in which his labour has been objectified, must rather be compelled to offer for sale as a commodity that very labour-power which exists only in his living body'.[10] The owner of labour power must have nothing to sell – nothing in the sense of nothing objective – other than the physical and intellectual qualities effectively realised in their activity.

What is necessary for someone to be able to sell use values, produced by them, other than their labour power? 'In order that a man may be able to sell commodities other than his labour-power, he must of course possess means of production, such as raw materials, instruments of labour, etc. . . . he requires also the means of subsistence.'[11] Marx could not say more clearly that what forces one into the position of being a seller of labour power is destitution: in order to be the owner and seller of labour power, in order to be a subjective depositary of labour power as an ensemble of purely intellectual and physical qualities, it is first of all necessary for one to be dispossessed of any objective possession, and at the same time of any relation with objectivity. It is necessary not just to no longer have an object to sell – i.e. use values in which labour power exists objectively – but also to be deprived of the means of producing such use values; in other words, it is necessary to be dispossessed of the objective conditions that permit the deployment of labour power as a vital activity. This 'loss of the object' must be radicalised to the point that it also entails the loss of one's means of subsistence, a loss which is decisive in the constraint to sell one's labour power. The lack of access to the means that permit one to live signifies the loss of the vital relationship to objectivity because the vital necessity to procure such means of subsistence is the original evidence in which a living thing recognises itself and its essential dependence with respect to those indispensable objects that enable it to maintain and perpetuate its proper life. As Marx puts it: 'just as on the first day of his appearance on the world's stage, man must still consume every day, before and while he produces'.[12] But the 'free worker' is equally deprived of this consumption as an essential condition of production, lack-

---

[10] Ibid., 272.
[11] Ibid.
[12] Ibid.

ing access to the vital objects that permit him to reproduce his or her vital forces of production. It is only possible to have access to the means of subsistence and consumption by having something to sell in exchange, but the owner of labour power has precisely nothing to exchange other than use values that have not yet been produced and which it is capable of producing: 'but no one, not even the producer of *Zukunftsmusik* [music of the future], can live on the products of the future, or on use-values whose production has not yet been completed'.[13] It is necessary to abolish this immersion in objectivity, the original relation to vital objects necessary for subsistence, in order to obtain 'free labour', that is to say, a subject constrained, in order to live, to sell not an object, even one to come, since it does not have the means to produce it, but its own 'aggregate of mental and physical capacities' that exists purely subjectively and uniquely as potential. The loss of all objectivity, complete destitution, the reduction to an impotence such that the individual no longer possesses the capacity to procure its proper means of subsistence – these are the elements indispensable to the fabrication of the subject possessed of a pure capacity of labour power. It is therefore under the conditions of its own reduction to subjective impotence that the individual is susceptible to entering into the process of the valorisation of capital.

It is thus that this economically produced pure subject – the simple owner of labour power – is also the subject of metaphysics, the pure subject for which objectivity is the other: the subject is characterised by a 'loss of the object' which is at the same time the loss of *its* own objects and its *own* objectivity, the objectivity of its existence as part of the objectivity of nature. This subject, which is only such because it is without its own object and at the same time disobjectified, can only be conceived and conceive itself in opposition to objectivity. Objectivity for it is always alienated: 'the relationship of the worker to the product of labour as an alien object ... is at the same time the relationship to the sensuous external world, to natural objects, as an alien world confronting him in hostile opposition'.[14] This relationship to objectivity as a fundamentally hostile element is itself only a manifestation of the 'poverty' and 'complete destitution' that characterise the subject's own labouring activity when it is comprised of a purely subjective activity. Posited as pure force of labour power, labour only exists as a non-objectified labour, as 'non-objectified itself' ('das Nichtgegenständliche selbst in objektiver Form').[15] Labour is non-objective, *Nichtgegenständliche*, in the sense

[13] Ibid. Translation modified.
[14] Marx, *Early Writings*, 327.
[15] Marx, *Grundrisse*, 296.

that the objective conditions of its own actuality are radically separate from it, as the property of another, which is capital: This 'purely subjective existence of labour, stripped of all objectivity', is also 'labour separated from all means and objects of labour'; in short, it is 'Labour as absolute poverty', this last aspect being conceived not only negatively as a lack of objectivity but also positively as the 'total exclusion of objective wealth'.[16] Marx adds that this non-objectivity is 'under the objective form' (*in objektiver Form*), in the sense that it is immediately under the non-mediated form of a natural and immediate being: as poverty and destitution, it is presented objectively under the form 'of the immediate existence of the individual itself'; more precisely, under the form of 'an objectivity coinciding with his immediate bodily existence'.[17] The infinitely impoverished and stripped-bare nature of work as the purely subjective form of a labour power without objectivity finds its own immediately objective manifestation in the form of an absolutely destitute individual reduced to his or her 'immediate body': purely subjective and non-objective (*nichtgegenständliche*) labour power is, in its objective form (*in objektiver Form*), the immediate body, the stripped and naked body of a living and working individual.

It is then obviously very tempting to think that this 'absolute poverty' is also what saves, that it is the condition for the conquest of the greatest wealth; since this conception of things was and often still is attributed to Marx, it is essential to note that here he takes the exact opposite position. The destitution of labour, separated from its own objective conditions and reduced to the absolute poverty of pure subjectivity, seems in effect, and paradoxically, to offer a way out. There is also here, as elsewhere, nothing surprising or paradoxical in a Hegelian reading of Marx: 'the purely subjective existence of labour' is also what Marx calls labour 'conceived as a negativity in relation to itself',[18] a negation of non-objective labour; labour as a negation of itself is what would permit the affirmation of labour in its positivity.

This is apparently the path that Marx takes: 'non-objective labour' is at the same time 'taken positively' as 'the non-objectified, hence non-objective, i.e. subjective existence of labour itself'.[19] If the emphasis is placed on the *non*-objectivity of labour, it is displaced and opened on to the non-*objectivity* of labour, which would lead to a positive concept of non-objectivity, which

[16] Ibid.
[17] Ibid.
[18] Ibid.
[19] Ibid.

is to say subjectivity. What is positive in this subjectivity conceived only negatively as the privation of objectivity, as the exclusion of the dimension of objectivity? Marx says in the first of the 'Theses on Feuerbach' that it is the idealists (Kant, Fichte, Hegel) who have grasped this positivity:[20] thinking completely positively and absolutely of subjectivity is an affirmation of activity (*Täglichkeit*). In the impotence, destitution and poverty of a nonobjective force, subjectivity thus becomes an absolutely affirmative and fully positive activity: 'Labour, not as an object, but as activity: not as value but as the living source of value . . . general wealth (in contrast to capital in which it exists objectively, as reality) as the general possibility of the same, which proves itself in action.'[21]

The question, however, is to know if this reversal of the subjective impotence of labour, separated from the objective conditions of its own valorisation, is a fully affirmative activity, creative of value; if it is a reversal which permits both the effective extraction of the value form and also its opposition to capital. Michael Hardt and Antonio Negri, for example, have claimed that in this passage from the *Grundrisse* Marx anticipated an evolution that we find ourselves at the centre of today, with the passage to the 'paradigm of immaterial production' in which there is an effective reversal of the destitution of subjective labour into the potential activity 'creative of social life itself'.[22] This does not, however, seem to be Marx's thesis, at least in the text in question, where we read the following:

> Thus, it is not at all contradictory, or, rather, the in-every-way mutually contradictory statements that labour is *absolute poverty as object*, on one side, and is, on the other side, the *general possibility* of wealth as subject and as activity, are reciprocally determined and follow from the essence of labour, such as it is *presupposed* by capital as its contradiction . . . and such as it, in turn, presupposes capital.[23]

What is Marx telling us here if not that labour understood as the subjective wealth creative activity is at the same time posited by capital as its opposite? In brief, the contradictory thesis of labour understood on the one hand as the absolute poverty of subjectivity reduced to labour power, and, on the other, as a subjectively positive and creative activity, articulates two sides of

---

[20] On this point see the chapter on Marx in our *L'etre et l'acte*.
[21] Marx, *Grundrisse*, 296.
[22] Hardt and Negri, *Multitude*, 146.
[23] Marx, *Grundrisse*, 296.

the same relation: work as purely subjective creative activity does not take us outside of the framework in which subjective impotence without an object can return to its opposite – the affirmation of subjective creative activity – without anything being fundamentally transformed.

9

Pure and Impure Activity

When the vital activity unique to humans is considered in terms of natural beings existing objectively in nature it is perhaps only unique in that it is an activity that produces objects. Such an activity can perhaps be judged inessential only from the point of view of a philosophy that starts from the place of the subject and that examines only the act by which the subject poses and affirms itself as subject. Importantly, 'in the act of establishing [objects]', Marx writes, humanity 'does not descend from its "pure activity" to the creation of objects; on the contrary, its objective product simply confirms its *objective* activity, its activity as the activity of an objective, natural being'.[1] Nothing is more natural and nothing is more necessary, for a being itself produced by nature and therefore engendered by natural objects, than engendering and producing in its turn naturally existing objects: 'It creates and establishes only objects because it is established by objects, because it is fundamentally nature.'[2] It is the essential break between passivity and activity that is overcome by Marx, as he demonstrates in the decisive and often remarked upon passage from the *1844 Manuscripts*: 'The domination of the objective essence within me, the sensuous outburst of my essential activity, is passion, which here becomes the activity of my being.'[3] For Marx, as for Hume, the 'mother of passions' is a passion for activity, a drive for activity;[4] it would not be false to call it a compulsory activity. The opposition of

---

[1] Marx, *Early Writings*, 389.
[2] Ibid.
[3] Ibid., 336.
[4] See Granel, 'David Hume, Le cynisme de la production', 315: 'activity does not rest on the metaphysical opposition of action and passion, but defines all of our passions in the essence (in their passions) as also forms of a mother-passion which is the passion of activity'. See also Didier Deleule (from whom Granel gets this concept of 'mother passion'), *Hume et la naissance du libéralisme politique*.

activity and passivity no longer makes sense for Spinoza, for whom the conception of human beings as part of nature certainly implies the affirmation of their natural passionate servitude, but also the thesis according to which, for the exact same reasons, the infinite power of nature is expressed in human beings as in every natural being under the form of a conatus, as that activity of persevering which, positively and for itself, produces a certain number of effects. In the same way, Marx could perhaps say that the human being considered as *Naturwesen*, that is, as a 'natural active being' endowed with 'natural' or 'vital' powers, is also 'a suffering, conditioned and limited being'.[5] This second aspect does not contradict the first to the extent that the essential and vital objects by which human beings are initially passively affected – in terms of a need and dependency with respect to something external – are also those which, in the activity of their appropriation or their production, become at the same time objects that are 'indispensable to the exercise and the confirmation of [their] essential powers'.[6] It is through the same external objects, both sensible and objective, that human beings also 'express their life' in an active manner productive of effects.

Marx thus rejoins Spinoza in the way in which he overcomes the opposition between activity and passivity: there is no pure passivity, but only a diminution of activity for a natural being that is active and acting, a being which is the expression in determined and particular form of the same activity of nature. But if there is no pure passivity, there is also no pure activity. Hence the criticism that Marx constantly makes of metaphysical concepts of the 'pure act' or 'pure activity': in 'the act of positing', he writes, human beings do not fall from 'pure activity' into the creation of objects.[7] Although he absolutely claims the point of view of activity in the first of the 'Theses on Feuerbach', and the new materialism he presents in *The German Ideology* as a materialism of practice places real activity at its centre – that is to say, the natural and social activity of human beings – despite this, or rather because of it, Marx is careful not to resuscitate any metaphysics of pure activity. His critique of the concept of the pure act or of pure activity is first of all addressed to Fichtean and Hegelian idealism, but also and overall to the young Hegelians, such as Hess who, in his *Philosophy of Action*, believes it is essential to borrow from the idealists the conception of the self or spirit as pure activity, unconditioned, infinite and therefore free. The text that is most clear on this point is a passage from *The German Ideology* con-

---

[5] Marx, *Early Writings*, 389.
[6] Ibid., 389–90.
[7] Ibid., 389.

cerning, not Hess, but another representative of 'true socialism', namely Karl Grün: 'We see here', Marx and Engels write, what the true socialists mean by 'free activity'; going on to explain that '[o]ur author imprudently reveals to us that free activity is activity which "is not determined by things external to us", i.e., actus purus, pure, absolute activity, which is nothing but activity and is in the last instance tantamount to the illusion of "pure thought". It naturally sullies the purity of this activity if it has a material basis and a material result.'[8] For a natural and objective being such as a human being, there is no activity which is not in one way or another determined by objects exterior to it: which, as Marx says, means that the objects that human beings depend on become the basis for the expression and exertion of the specific activity of their natural being. It is from here that we get to the Spinozist distinction between 'operating' and 'acting':[9] if a finite mode always begins by being determined in its activity by something other than itself, and therefore begins by 'operating', nothing restricts its capacity to increase its power to act, and, by integrating into its operation the processes of reason (which begins with the formation of common notions), to begin to truly act, that is, to deploy an activity which stems from only its own nature.

It is, then, in critiquing any metaphysics of the *actus purus* that Marx rejoins Spinoza. Because it would be an error to attribute to Spinoza a thought of the pure act on the pretext that substance is nothing other than an infinite power that is absolutely in action, with nothing remaining in the state of simple potential, as purely possible, which would be a necessary mark of limitation or impotence. Because one cannot think with respect to Spinoza a pure act which would be independent of production itself: the infinite activity of substance is only 'pure' in the sense that it is perfectly immanent to production itself. In other words, *natura naturans* and *natura naturata* are identical, they are the one and only nature considered from two different points of view. The active principle of natural productivity is not left separated and isolated in its purity from the activity it produces, that is to say, from the effective putting-to-work of natural production.

A being that is a part of nature can only be at the same time a being that is affected in many ways by other parts of nature: put differently, it is a being always already engaged in affective relations with other parts of nature, a

---

[8] Marx and Engels, *The German Ideology*, 492.
[9] On this distinction that permits Spinoza to overcome the opposition between passivity and activity (passivity only exists as diminished activity, and this is what designates precisely the concept of operation), see Macherey, 'Action et operation: sur la signification éthique du *De Deo*', and Tosel, 'Qu'est-ce qu'agir pour un mode fini selon Spinoza?'

being which is therefore that which it is only through the relations of affect that it enters into with other natural beings. It is for this reason that human beings are essentially social beings. Because of this, Spinoza contests any solution predicated on a division between the state of nature and civil society: the latter is only the continuation of the former, and the natural state, the natural situation, is always already a social situation; each part of nature and each finite mode, as much under the attribute of thought as of extension, is defined by the relations it enters into with others. This originally relational dimension of human life as a being and part of nature reappears in Marx in the affirmation that 'the human essence of nature exists only for social man; for only here does nature exist as bond with other men'.[10] Contrary to all ideas of humanity as an exception to the general order of nature, Marx posits that, by the intermediary of human beings, nature is reunited with nothing other than itself, in the same way that, by its relation to nature, humanity is reunited with nothing other than itself. Marx adds that humanity can only reunite with itself through the intermediary of nature because its relation with nature is a social relation: it is because humanity is social that it is related to nature. For human beings there is no individual relation to nature; all human relation to nature is a social relation. Thus the 'subject' of the vital human activity of the appropriation and transformation of nature can never ever be an individual or a singular human being, but is solely the human species, and therefore all of humanity, or human society.

One can thus understand why in every case Marx immediately assimilates 'human existence' and 'social existence', speaking of 'his human, i.e. social existence':[11] to the same extent that the existence of human beings is naturally social, their essence is generic and their consciousness is at the same time the consciousness of species. Hence Marx can also write: 'My universal consciousness is only the theoretical form of that whose living form is the real community, society . . .'.[12] Which means that, to the exact extent that the vital activity of humanity is a necessarily social activity, human consciousness is the consciousness of the species. As Marx also says: 'As species-consciousness man confirms his real social life and merely repeats in thought his actual existence.'[13] In other words, if the species consciousness takes the inverse form of the consciousness of a singular self, if the consciousness of the species contradicts itself in the priority it ascribes to the form of self-

[10] Marx, *Early Writings*, 349.
[11] Ibid.
[12] Ibid., 350.
[13] Ibid.

consciousness, it is because actual social life has itself taken on the negative and inverted form of a divided society, labour has been divided into multiple factors, private property has been instituted, and social life has thus been reduced to competitive relations between individuals. The individual consciousness of a singular self is the contradictory form of generic consciousness that is inevitably engendered by an actual social life founded on what we have come to call 'possessive individualism'. This also explains how it is that human consciousness cannot be anything other than the immediate form of consciousness of a singular self within a form of social organisation that abstracts the existence of the individual from society, and society itself from nature.

There are for Marx two elements or two parallel series: one could be called 'real existence', that is to say the element in which the natural activity of human beings is deployed as a social activity, and the other is the element of 'generic consciousness', that is to say thought. The latter element could be said to be repetition of the first, which is not to say that it is a copy or still a reflection. It is the one and same essential reality which is expressed in one part in the social life of human beings as part of nature, and in the other part ideally in thought or in generic consciousness. For Marx as for Spinoza, thought is more vast than consciousness, and consciousness of the species is more vast than the consciousness of the self, such that it is possible to say that this is the place of the unconscious. However, for Spinoza this unconscious of thought relates directly to the unknown of the body,[14] while for Marx the unconscious of thought is first of all the unknown of society: the social forces deployed in the activity of social appropriation can be seen and lived as unknown forces, and thus as strange and hostile, without at the same time, in the series of ideas, consciousness of the species or thought itself being reduced to the consciousness of the singular self. It follows therefore that the reconquest of the unknown human forces at work in the appropriation and social transformation of nature is necessarily accompanied by a reconquest of the unconscious of thought, and therefore by a going beyond of the subjective figure of consciousness. This reconquest passes through the expansion of consciousness of the self to the dimension of the consciousness of the species, which entails, in the ideal attribute of

---

[14] See Deleuze, *Spinoza: Practical Philosophy*, 18–19: 'In short, the model of the body, according to Spinoza, does not imply any devaluation of thought in relation to extension, but, much more important, a devaluation of consciousness in relation to thought: a discovery of the unconscious, of an *unconscious of thought* just as profound as *the unknown of the body.*'

thought, a desubjectivation of thought that signifies at the same time, in the element of actual social life, a desubjectification of human beings. It is not a matter of saying that for Spinoza the unconscious is individual, while for Marx it is collective, that the Spinozist unconsciousness is individual while the Marxist unconsciousness is social; rather, it is necessary to affirm that the unconscious escapes the alternative of the individual or the collective in that it is primarily relational;[15] that is to say, it is structurally linked to the relationships of composition, recomposition, decomposition, agreement and disagreement between natural elements – which is nothing other than what Marx meant by the social.

It is necessary to take the measure of the philosophical radicality of Marx's thesis of the unity of man and nature, that is, of their identity: for Marx it was never a matter of showing how two separate and distinct beings – man as 'subject' on the one side and nature as 'object' on the other – are reunited in the course of a process named 'history'. The theme of the unity of humanity and nature appears in Marx without any mythic character, neither that of a lost origin nor that of an end to come in a utopian perspective:[16] the unity of humanity and nature is the same thing as what Marx calls 'essential reality', that is to say, the being of that which exists. In order to understand this it is necessary to return to the thesis that 'man is immediately a natural being'[17] and grasp that the most important term in this thesis is 'immediately' – which to our knowledge Gerard Granel is the first to have clearly seen. 'The origin and centre of the Marxist ontology of 1844', he writes, 'can be expressed in the idea that human beings have no relation with nature in which each would be the other term of the relation, so that both would be abstractly situated as something undetermined before entering into a relationship'.[18] In order to better understand the sense and the ontological opening of the thought of Marx, it is necessary to begin on the side of the Marxist, but not Marxian, theme of the relation of human beings and nature. It is necessary to return to the passage already cited from the 'Notes on Adolph Wagner's "Lehrbuch der politischen Ökonomie"': '[human beings]

[15] This is the precise point underscored by Jean-Marie Vaysse in L'inconscient des modernes, 73. 'It is a false problem', he writes, 'to ask if the unconscious is individual or collective, because it is first of all interrelational, as much as the variation of differential relations in a system that functions as a distribution of singularities. In other words, the unconscious is structural.'

[16] On this point see the indispensable work of Schmidt, The Concept of Nature in Marx, particularly chapter four: 'Utopia and the Relation between Man and Nature'.

[17] Marx, Early Writings, 389. Translation modified.

[18] Granel, 'L'ontologie marxiste de 1844 et la question de la "coupure"', 185.

begin, like every animal, by *eating, drinking*, etc., that is, not by "finding themselves" in a relationship, but *actively behaving*, availing themselves of certain things of the outside world by action, and thus satisfying their needs. (They start, then, with production.)'[19] This passage not only says that the practical and active relation of human beings to nature is primary and prior to the theoretical relation (which is what we have taken it to say up to now), it also and above all makes it clear that human beings and nature find themselves in a relation in which one term stands in for the other: not as 'a term which stands for itself in front of the other' but on the contrary that 'the one and the other are only . . . in the original character of their being the one in the other (or quite simply the being of one in the other)'.[20] For Marx there only exists this being that is the being in one another of nature and humanity; this coappearance of the one and the other also describes the essence of humanity, insofar as its essence is in the essence of nature itself, that is, the same essence of nature insofar as it is the being of humanity. If Marx invokes here the living animal in general it is not to reduce the human perspective to this, just as it is not to reduce metaphysically the essence of humanity to an animal 'plus an unspecified something', for example as 'rational animal'. It is rather, first of all, to oppose the appearance of human beings in nature to any thought of a subject-object, but it is also moreover to affirm that human beings are the only ones who have responded to the essence of nature to the extent to which, as a being of nature, that is to say, as that which exists through nature, they return to their own being which is in question. Marx ultimately asserts only one thing: that nature is the very name of being in general; 'that being is, and that this is the very being of man'.[21]

It is a matter of an 'ontology of immanence' which, as with Spinoza, can perhaps at the same time be thought of as an 'ontology without theology'.[22] Thus we are brought, finally, to the question of atheism. If the formulas of the 'Introduction to the Critique of Hegel's Philosophy of Right' in which Marx reclaims an atheism that could be qualified as militant are well known, then what is less well known[23] is the critique of atheism made in the *1844 Manuscripts* which qualifies it as an 'abstraction'.[24] There, Marx places

---

[19] Marx, 'Notes on Adolph Wagner's "Lehrbuch der politischen Ökonomie"'.
[20] Granel, 'L'ontologie marxiste de 1844 et la question de la "coupure"', 186.
[21] Ibid.
[22] We borrow this expression from Jean-Marie Vaysse, who has used it in relation to Spinoza, in *L'inconscient des modernes*, 58.
[23] The exception is Granel, 'L'ontologie marxiste de 1844 et la question de la "coupure"', 188–91.
[24] Marx, *Early Writings*, 349.

himself philosophically at the point where atheism 'no longer has any meaning'.[25] The sense proposed by Marx is one in which atheism has become in his eyes a secondary problem which it is useless to reclaim. 'Atheism', he writes, 'is a negation of God, through which negation it asserts the existence of man';[26] the atheism of Feuerbach for example, still posits the existence of God even if it is only to negate it and through this intermediary return to humanity as it has reappropriated its own essence initially alienated in God. God becomes for atheism an intermediary, an essential middle term, since it is only in passing through it that humanity can return to what is essential to it. The humanism of Feuerbach, as much as it is an atheism, is still in essence theological: it returns to theology most notably with the central role that the concept of mediation plays in the middle term and the intermediary. Marx's critique focuses precisely on this concept of mediation that is as much Hegelian as it is theological. In his notes on James Mills' *Elements of Political Economy*, written at the same time as the *1844 Manuscripts*, Marx explains that it is inevitable that 'this mediator must become a veritable God', to the extent that 'the mediator is the real power over that with which he mediates me'.[27] This would certainly describe the figure of Christ as the mediator between humanity and God, but it also describes the role of money as general equivalent, as universal mediator. As soon as the process of mediation is no longer immanent and is attributed to a mediator external to the terms of the relation, the mediated terms no longer have value by themselves, but only with regard to and in relation to the one who mediates them. Hence the importance of the concept of immediacy in the thesis according to which 'man is immediately a natural being (*Naturewesen*)':[28] humanity is the being of existence, but it is so above all immediately, and therefore without intermediary. Positing an intermediary, even to negate it afterwards, between humanity and the totality of being that it is, is to immediately open a breach which theology never ceases to rush in to fill. Marx also asserts clearly the point of view of an a-theological ontology which paradoxically dispenses with atheism, making it philosophically useless: 'the essentiality of man and of nature (*die Wesenhaftigkeit*), man as the existence of nature for man and nature as the existence of man for man, has become practically and sensuously perceptible, the question of an alien being, a being above nature and man – a question which implies an admission of

---

[25] Ibid., 357.
[26] Ibid.
[27] Ibid., 260.
[28] Ibid., 389. Translation modified.

the unreality of nature and of man – has become impossible in practice',[29] even in the (Feuerbachian) mode of an alien being that is posited in order to be negated. Here 'the essentiality of man and of nature' renders poorly the term *Wesenhaftigkeit*, by which Marx expresses the essential coappearance of humanity and nature, which is to say the immediate coappearance of this singular being that humanity is and the very being of beings. The one and the other are immediately in the one in the other, they have each other (the verb 'to have', '*haben*', is present in 'Wesen-haft-igkeit') in the sense that the immanent and mutual relation of each is just as integral to the existence of each as what is essential or substantial, to the exclusion of all transcendence, of all exteriority or mediation. Humanity is therefore, according to Marx, the being for which its very being and existence is a question, the being which therefore, in its being, has to answer for being itself, and who answers for it effectively, that is to say actively, by increasing as much as it can its power to individually and collectively affirm the infinite productivity of nature itself.

[29] Ibid., 357.

Conclusion: Metaphysics and Production

> This is what Spinoza calls Nature: a life no longer lived on the basis of need, in terms of means and ends, but according to a production, a productivity, a potency, in terms of causes and effects.
>
> Gilles Deleuze, Spinoza: Practical Philosophy

One of the constant points of reference for Heidegger when he interrogates the field of human activity is that he lets himself be guided by the Greek language and therefore by the immediate relation with *pragma* and *pragmata*, that is to say, with things insofar as they are useful and utilisable. He also translates *praxis* by *Handlung*, which is distinguished by the presence of the hand (*der Hand*) insofar as it manipulates and utilises things. This reduction of *praxis* to a preoccupation with things insofar as they are manipulable and usable is manifest in *Being and Time*, notably in §15, where Heidegger writes that 'the Greeks had an appropriate term for "things", *pragmata*, that is, that with which one has to do in taking care of things in association (praxis)'.[1] In referring *praxis* immediately to *pragmata*, however, Heidegger is perhaps led to deny *praxis* any autonomy with respect to *poiesis*: the latter appears to be the central category through which human activity is understood, at least insofar as that activity is undertaken and conducted in a manner that could be described as inauthentic. According to Heidegger, this reduction of *praxis* to *poiesis* is not his doing, but that of metaphysics itself, insofar as it naively returns to a meaning of action as the quality through which human beings relate to the world productively as a world of things that are useful and manipulable, that is, to things produced which are capable of being used in order to further production. Hence, according to Heidegger, the analysis of this productive comportment is the analysis of a comportment that has

---

[1] Heidegger, *Being and Time*, 64.

determined the history and orientation of western metaphysics, and the totality of this history, up to today, that is to say, up to the epoch of the achievement of metaphysics in the world of technology, the world of the productive control of the being of everything.

Heidegger's 'existential analytic of Dasein' breaks radically with such a comprehension of human activity immediately determined by the productive comportment of Dasein. Following Jean-Luc Nancy, one can perhaps amend this to say that, according to Heidegger, 'in Dasein, it is about giving sense to the fact of being – or more exactly, in Dasein the fact of being is: to make sense; on the condition that this "making" is not a "producing", and that it is, precisely, to act, or to conduct oneself'. What is particularly interesting is Nancy's proposal to translate '*die Handlung*' by 'conduct',[2] which makes it possible to understand Heidegger's effort to situate himself outside of the metaphysical couple of *praxis* (action) and *poeisis* (production): conduct is for Heidegger an original category, prior to the distinction between conduct as action or conduct as production. It is therefore essentially in and through 'conduct' that Dasein responds to the sense of being; productive or poetic conduct are the means by which it responds. Productive conduct is the conduct that prevents responding to the meaning of being since it decides that meaning in advance by reducing it to the one and only sense of being-produced, that is to say, to the sense of being as presence and subsistence.[3]

The phenomenological description of productive conduct or of the comportment of the producer that Heidegger gives in *The Basic Problems of Phenomenology* demonstrates in effect that there are certain major categories which have been, in their elaboration, determined by this comportment. The sense of metaphysical concepts as decisive as *eidos*, *hupokeimenon*, or *ousia* (to name just a few) has been definitely elaborated as a function of the productive nature of Dasein and of the pre-comprehension of the sense of being that Heidegger inherits. Thus, as he writes of *eidos*: 'The thing is produced by looking to the anticipated look of what is to be produced by shaping, forming. It is this anticipated look of the thing, sighted beforehand,

---

[2] It is in his article 'Heidegger' (695–701) that Nancy proposes to translate 'die Handlung' by 'conduct' (rather than action) and 'handeln' by 'conducting oneself' rather than acting. Nancy's text entitled 'L'ethique originaire de Heidegger' in *La pensée dérobée* is a more developed version of this article. I am thankful to Olivier Tinland to having made me aware of this particularly enlightening text.

[3] The only conduct that, according to Heidegger, permits one to respond to the sense of being, the only sensible conduct, that is to say the sole sensitive conduct, is thought or thinking: The 'Letter on Humanism' explains that only 'thought truly acts'.

that the Greeks mean ontologically by eidos, idea.'[4] Or with *hupokeimenon* (the substrate, the subject in the sense of *subjectum*, that which is under – sub – or before 'das Vor-liegende'): 'but to *pro*-duce, to place-*here*, *Her*-stellen, means at the same time to bring into the narrower or wider circuit of the accessible, here, to this place, to the Da, so that the produced being *stands for itself* on its own account and remains able to be found there and to *lie-before-there* as *something established stably for itself*. This is the source of the Greek term hupokeimenon, that which lies-before.'[5] And finally *ousia* (substance): 'The basic concept of ousia, in contrast, lays more stress on the producedness of the produced in the sense of things disposably present at hand [*vorhanden*].'[6] It is thus that 'the chief ancient determinations for the thingness or reality of a being originate in productive activity, the comprehension of being by way of production'.[7] It is also the source for principal modern determinations of reality (essence, existence) to the extent they emerge from this productive activity: the two concepts of *essentia* and *existential* (effectively stems from effectuation, just as *actualitas* is product of an *agere*) 'are derived from an understanding of being that comprehends beings with respect to an actualizing or, as we say generally, to a *productive comportment of the Dasein*'.[8] This is the meaning of *essentia*, which is a translation of *ousia* and inherits the sense of being as 'being disposable', treated as that which 'which belongs to it due to its having been produced';[9] but it is also the sense of *existentia* which, 'conceived as actualization and actuality', 'returns to *agere*, as *agens*, and *energein*',[10] 'apprehended as actualitas, actuality, and hence with regard to actus, agere',[11] the sense of this *actum* being precisely an action which is effectuated, actualised, which is to say a being that is produced.

These analyses in the course of 1927, overlapping with the publication of *Being and Time* that same year, are evidently decisive for everything that follows in the Heideggerian interpretation of the history of metaphysics: they make it possible to see this history as having been determined from its beginnings by the productive comportment of Dasein and by the comprehension of being as presence, subsistence and being usable or being-present-at hand,

---

[4] Heidegger, *The Basic Problems of Phenomenology*, 106.
[5] Ibid., 108.
[6] Ibid., 109.
[7] Ibid., 105.
[8] Ibid.
[9] Ibid., 109.
[10] Ibid., 100.
[11] Ibid., 130.

inasmuch as this comprehension is characteristic of the everyday average of Dasein. One can also see from this that our era of global production can be understood as the epoch of the becoming-world of metaphysics: from the beginning, the fate of metaphysics was linked with production and vice versa. The achievement of the Moderns came under a metaphysics of the will by which everything is essentially calculable and manipulable, made available by and for production, thus metaphysics has done nothing else but reveal the link that connected it from the beginning with the productive activity of Dasein.

It is remarkable that Heidegger, in a text of 1939/40 titled 'Κοινόν: Out of the History of Being',[12] describes 'communism' as an historical configuration marked by a metaphysics that has as its foundation 'the interpretation of being as effective and efficacy and, in the last instance, as power'.[13] By communism, Heidegger does not understand the political regime or economic system that would claim this name and that he would have been able to see in Stalin's USSR in 1939. 'Communism', he explains, 'is no mere form of state, nor simply a kind of political worldview, but rather the *metaphysical constitution* in which the humankind of modernity finds itself as soon as the consummation of modernity begins its final stage.'[14] Communism as the ultimate stage or last stage of modernity thus also concerns those social and political regimes that would claim to be capitalist as well. If, in this text, Heidegger does not go into the roots of communism, does not explore it further than an examination of the modern metaphysics of the will from British philosophy (most notably Hobbes) up to Rousseau and Hegel, it is clear that the 'communism' of the worldly becoming of metaphysics, in as much as it is interpreted as calculable and manipulable, is the ascendence of something much older, whose origins are to be found in ancient metaphysics insofar as its principal concepts have been elaborated, as we have seen, from the productive attitude of Dasein. It is this sense that Heidegger reminds us of when he remarks that 'this malleability (*die Machsamkeit*[15]) enjoins beings into the unlimited and constant securing of their presence; in such malleability the figure, specific to modern metaphysics, of the *energéia* and the idea that metaphysically characterizes modernity shows itself'.[16] Note that in this pas-

---

[12] Published in English in *The History of Beyng*.
[13] According to Jean-Marie Vaysse, in his discussion of this text by Heidegger. Vaysse, *Totalité et Finitude: Spinoza et Heidegger*, 226.
[14] Heidegger, *The History of Beyng*, 175.
[15] We propose 'malleability' for *Machsamkeit* to distinguish it from the German word *Machbarkeit* that Heidegger does not use here.
[16] Ibid., 158.

sage the analysis of Κοινόν and the *History of Beyng* mobilises all the possible derivations of the verb *machen* (making), all approaching systematically *machen* of *die Macht* (power or ability): communism as the ultimate phase of modernity is comprised of the reign of '*Machenschaft*', 'that which possesses the character of making' or 'machination'. Heidegger explains that 'in machination, being's falling off in the commencement into the constancy of its essential absencing attains the supreme corruption of its essence'.[17] The character of making or machination is therefore 'a denomination of the essence of being': it is that which is suitable when we arrive at the last stage of the forgetting of being, its forgetting in the sense of being present and subsistent, which is at one and the same time both the result and the condition of the activity of production, that is to say, of 'making'. In this ultimate stage, Being is subordinated to an 'augmentation of power' which 'intensifies its essence to the extreme of machination', to a process which conducts it to the rule of *Machenschaft*, that is to say, to communism as the reign of making and machination: 'Power's empowering into the unconditional aspect of machination and from out of the latter is the essence of communism.'[18] Here it is necessary to be precise: the concept of communism is 'thought from the history of Being'; it acts therefore as a concept that is neither 'political' nor 'sociological', which does not stem from a vision of the world, whether anthropological or metaphysical. Communism here 'is conceived as the ordering of beings as such and as a whole that marks the historical era as that of the consummation and therefore the end of all metaphysics'.[19] In this end, Being reigns as *Machenschaft* (machination) and is said ontically as *Machsamkeit*, as 'malleability'; in both cases there is a deployment of a *Macht*, a power, moreover a power of infinite mastery or unconditional domination which has no other role than its proper *Ermächtigung*, that is, the reinforcement of its own proper power of domination and mastery. In this process of *Ermächtigung* without limit, capitalism and communism, considered as 'world powers' confused in their identity, manifest their common essence in war, which they elevate to a global level: world war or total war is nothing other than the deployment and development of *Ermächtigung* in its most immediately visible, mundane existence. Beginning in production, metaphysics thus achieves in total war the deployment of its historical essence.

However, what does Heidegger understand by production? Moreover, how to understand production according to the term he adopts in 1939: 'making'.

[17] Ibid.
[18] Ibid., 162.
[19] Ibid.

The course of 1927, *The Basic Problems of Phenomenology*, offers some important indications on this point. Production consists, according to Heidegger, as the placing in presence of a subject with a being, and reciprocally a being with a subject. In 'the understanding of being that belongs to productive comportment and thus in the understanding of what does not need to be produced . . . there can grow the understanding of a being which is extant in itself *before* all production and for all further production'.[20] However, such a way of encountering being, considered as a product and a completed result in itself, necessitates the existence of another being against which it comes to be or in relation to which it clashes. To say that what exists, exists as a product, as something completed, is to say that it actually exists but that this actuality stems from and returns to an actor (the productive actor) and therefore an agent: 'the verbal definition of existentia already made clear that *actualitas* refers back to an *acting* on the part of some indefinite subject'; 'the apparently objective interpretation of being as actualitas . . . refers back to the subject . . . in the sense of a relation to our Dasein as acting Dasein, or, to speak more precisely, as a . . . *productive* Dasein'.[21] Productive behaviour thus harbours in itself from the outset the subject/object relationship: the existence that is called 'effective' or 'actual' of the produced being returns to the productive activity of a subject, just as the produced being's character of manipulability and disposability returns to 'something for which, as it were, it *comes to be before the hand*, at hand, to be handled'.[22] In other words, in its orientation, at 'least implicitly',[23] and thus for its initial formulation in Antiquity, and in its function in 'everyday life' or in the 'everyday behavior'[24] that is productive comportment, metaphysics was already preparing its own fulfilment as the metaphysics of subjectivity.

This conception of production as immediately inscribed at the centre of the subject/object relation seems convincing. However, it is challenged by at least two authors who have in common (among the other things we have considered) the fact that Heidegger never entered into dialogue with them: namely Spinoza and Marx. It is also certain that these are two central thinkers of production in the history of philosophy, and that Heidegger almost never addresses either of them in his characterisation of metaphysics as the metaphysics of production: there is no mention of Marx and only one

---

[20] Heidegger, *The Basic Problems of Phenomenology*, 116.
[21] Ibid., 101.
[22] Ibid.
[23] Ibid., 145.
[24] Ibid.

allusive mention of Spinoza in *The Basic Problems of Phenomenology*. Spinoza is however the philosopher who posits an infinite productivity at the foundation of being in general and the totality of being in particular: the power (*potentia*) of God, that is to say his essence,[25] is the power by which 'all things are and act'.[26] God, according to Spinoza, is an infinitely productive force eternally and absolutely active, a force that exists only in and through the immanence of the infinity of the things it produces. If the modes as products can be understood as objects it is because they have an objective reality, but not by an opposition to a subject, since God is not a subject that would be in opposition to objects: God is not the subject of production because he does not exist apart from the objectivity of his production and is absolutely immanent to it. In the same way that God is not the subject of production, but exists in the immanence of his own infinitely objective production, the things produced – what Spinoza calls 'modes' – are not in a relation of subjects to objects, but in a relation of things produced to things produced, objects to objects. None of these things possesses in relation to the others any sort of ontological privilege that permits them to be placed in the position of the subject, which exists in illusory form in the case of the human mode.

Spinoza and Marx lead us to suspect that, when Heidegger speaks of 'production', it is not production in itself that is at stake but a form that it has historically taken in terms of work. Presupposing the 'labour form' of production, Heidegger always analyses the latter as a function of the former. The opposition between a subjective productive actor on the one hand, and the products and objective means of this subjective activity on the other, is certainly a characteristic of the labour form of production, but it remains to be seen if this form expresses the essence of production, or if, on the contrary, it represents a fundamental break with this essence. The framework of the labour form of production is led to posit, as its foundation or base, the subject as a stable support for productive activity, and it follows that its opposite, the object, is inert matter – brought out of its inertia only by 'the flames of the power of living labour',[27] by the objective means used by the work, and finally by the objective product of the work, the object as a work or product. Heidegger is therefore not wrong to establish a link between, on the one hand, the understanding of the being of man as subject, and, on the other hand, the deployment of this subject's activity in the form of work, insofar as

---

[25] Spinoza, *Ethics* I, 34 Dem.; *CWS* I, 439.
[26] Ibid.
[27] Marx, *Grundrisse*, 454.

CONCLUSION   117

this form supposes the confrontation of the subject with objectivity, as well as the desire for mastery and domination of the first over the second. The error would be to think that work can express the sense of production, that the labour form can represent the accomplished form of production. Spinoza and Marx make it possible to understand that the labour form dissimulates, obscures and betrays the true sense of production.

The fundamental point these two philosophers have in common is their being at one and the same time thinkers of production and radical critics of subjectivity – two elements that are completely indissociable. While Heidegger considers the modern metaphysics of subjectivity as the completion and accomplishment of an approach than consists, from Greek philosophy onwards, in taking the productive comportment of humanity as the implicit guiding thread into the sense of being, Spinoza and Marx demonstrate on the contrary that a thought of production leads to the removal of subjectivity from its foundational role. Neither Spinoza nor Marx start from the subject: the former begins from *substance* and understands it as the infinite activity of production, that is, as the absolute unity of producing (*natura naturans*) and of product (*natura naturata*), as the complete immanence of production in the infinity of things produced; the latter begins not from the production as the activity of one or several subjects, but from the *ensemble* of the *relations* of production, a productive industry that is at the same time a process of individuation. In neither case is production thought from the subject: for both Spinoza and for Marx there is a production that exceeds all subjectivity, a production which has always already preceded, englobed and exceeded every subjective formation, engendering subjectivity as a secondary and derived aspect. Whether thinking of production as the infinite productivity of substance – which, in its immanence to the infinity of things produced, is demonstrated to be not at all a subject (the latter being conceived as that which precedes or supports the things that are produced, or as the term by which they are assembled) – or thinking of production as primarily an ensemble of *relations* that precede, condition and determine the formation of individually productive positions, both Spinoza and Marx understand and illustrate that production is never assignable to any foundational subject, that it is the basis of everything without being the act of a founding subject.

These two theses – production as the productivity of nature and production as the ensemble of relations of production – refer to each other and are completed by the shared theoretical position that lies at the core of the thought of both Spinoza and Marx: that of a radical critique of the modern philosophy of subjectivity. The Marxist thesis according to which production is always already the ensemble of the relations of production can also be understood as Spinozist insofar as, for Spinoza, what exists can only be described as relations. What actually exists? Individuals. What is an individual? It is a body composed of other bodies which are also composed as such, and so on to infinity.[28] What is it that makes these different bodies assemble in an ensemble such that they form a larger body that can be considered as an individual? The Spinozist response to this question consists in rejecting any internal or finalist organisation and contending that, in precise circumstances and in a determined environment, an external and purely mechanical constraint is exercised in such a way that certain bodies are arranged with others, communicating their movements in a manner that engenders a certain composed body, that is to say, an individual:

> When a number of bodies, whether of the same or of different size, are so constrained[29] by other bodies that they lie upon one another, or if they so move, whether with the same degree or different degrees of speed, that they communicate their motions to each other in a certain fixed manner, we shall say that those bodies are united with one another and that they all together compose one body or individual, which is distinguished from the others by this union of bodies.[30]

It is sufficient for these circumstances to change, for the environment to be modified, for this external constraint on the composition of parts to cease, and for the individual, the composed body, to disaggregate and decompose. The unity of the individual is thus conjunctural and transitory: far from starting from an individual essence capable of organising the parts that compose the individual, it is on the contrary necessary to explain the genesis of the individual from the existence of conjunctural relations and relations of reciprocity between bodies. It is the existence of conjunctural relations, and of the external and mechanical constraint exercised by the milieu on bodies and by bodies themselves on each other, that together cause the provisional composition of the individual. These relations of reciprocal constraint and

---

[28] This applies to all bodies; the human body is only more compounded than others, that is to say, composed of more bodies: 'The human body is composed of a great many individuals of different natures, each of which is highly composite.' Spinoza, *Ethics* II, 13 Post. I; *CWS* I, 462.

[29] We modify here the translation of B. Pautrat: the Latin is *coercentur*, which is better rendered by 'being constrained' ('être contraints') than 'being pressed' (être presses) [Translator's note: Edwin Curley's translation of the *Ethics* makes the same choice.]

[30] Spinoza *Ethics* II, 13 Def.; *CWS* I, 460.

mutual convenience are therefore primary, and are what constitute the composition of parts that engenders an individual.

At this point it might appear that we are far from Marx. Nevertheless, the modalities of aggregation of the diversity of bodies in an individual are the same as those of the aggregation of individuals themselves in a society. The physics of bodies that leads Spinoza to a 'social physics' rests on a thesis that can also be found in Marx, according to which, in human societies as in natural bodies, relations of reciprocal constraint and mutual correspondence are primary and determinant. The primacy of relations is affirmed in the sixth of the 'Theses on Feuerbach': 'the human essence is no abstraction inherent in each single individual (*kein dem einelnen Individuum inwohnendes Abstraktum*). In its reality it is the ensemble of the social relations (*das ensemble der gesellschaftlichen Verhältnisse*).'[31] Marx would say that a human essence separated from individuals is an abstraction; thus he excludes the so-called 'realist' position that would posit the real and separate existence of essences. But he also excludes the possibility of the human essence being 'an internal, dumb generality'[32] inherent to each individual taken separately and abstractly from others: this would then exclude the so-called 'nominalist' position, which claims that only individuals exist, and that an essence is disengaged from them only by an abstraction. It would, according to Marx, exclude from the beginning any subject as the ultimate guarantee of identity before differences or after them, any subject that would be the universal itself posited as the ultimate support and foundation for the specific differences of individuals, and any subject posited in each individual and inherent to each, identified by its abstraction from individual differences. Thus, in one singular gesture, Marx sets aside the subjectivity conceived by both Ancients and Moderns.

But where is the human essence if it is neither beyond individuals nor in them, if it is neither a general essence under which the specific and individual differences are subsumed, nor a general essence lodged in the individuals, inherent in them? If it is not a matter of thinking of the human essence as the substantial support of individual differences, nor of individual humans as subjective supports of the human essence, how is it possible to think this essence? Marx's response is that there is no possible solution other than thinking in a relational manner. Only a relational kind of thought makes it possible to go beyond both ancient substantialism and modern subjectivism. It is necessary to say that the human essence does not exist outside of the

---

[31] Marx, *Early Writings*, 423.
[32] Ibid.

relations between humans; that it is solely in these relations that it exists effectively and actually. This is what human beings are essentially: they are in the *social relations* that they enter into with each other. The essence of human beings lies in the 'commerce' (*Verkehr*) of human beings; in other words, the human essence is not before individual humans, nor is it beyond them, even less is it in each of them – it is nowhere else than between them. The essence of human beings is, according to Marx, an ensemble of that which passes between them; this ensemble includes both the matter of exchange (its contents or the things exchanged) and its form (the manner in which they are exchanged, the modalities and frames of exchange). To which it is necessary to add that the ensemble of that which passes between human beings is a determining ensemble in the sense that in each instance humans are what they are only in virtue of what they exchange (the content) and how it is exchanged between them (the form): individuals do not pre-exist the exchange, they only become individuals in and through the exchange; the exchange and the relations between them are what constitute them. The individuals depend therefore, constitutively and ontologically, on the ensemble of relations of exchange through which they emerge as individuals at the edge of these relations and through the spaces created between them. It is not just that this 'ontology of relation'[33] constitutes a remarkable point of comparison between Marx and Spinoza (for both, we have seen, individuals depend constitutively on the relations between the parts of which they are composed and on their own relations with other parts of nature); it is also that, for each of them, this central aspect of their theoretical apparatus makes possible their critique of the modern philosophical paradigm of the foundational subject.

If one asks now what, for Marx, is the content of exchange, or the matter of the relations, one is initially tempted to say that what matters are the things exchanged. But this would be to fail to see that, in the Marxist concept of relations, it is the exchange or the commerce itself that is more important, in the sense that the object of exchange is not essentially things, rather, the object of commerce between men is first of all productive activity itself.[34] Here the ontology of relation is completed in an 'ontology of activity'.[35] In the exchange of the products of this activity, it is first of all

[33] Balibar, *The Philosophy of Marx*, 32.
[34] See notably this passage from *The Holy Family*: 'the object as being for man, as the objectified being of man, is at the same time the existence of man for other men, his human relation to other men, the social relation of man to man'. Marx and Engels, *The Holy Family*, 60.
[35] We use this expression in our book *L'être et l'acte* (but Guy Haarscher had already

the productive activity itself that the individuals themselves reciprocally confirm and mutually constitute. However, in the exchange of activity, they also express and manifest an activity, a power of acting, that is constitutive of their being and that is nothing other than the nature which they are part of, or intensive degrees of. If the essence of individuals is nothing other than their own activity, or the power to act that they express in the productive relationships they establish with each other, and if these individuals cannot be conceived otherwise than as parts of nature, then their own productive activity is nothing more in its essence than the activity of nature itself: 'in the physical and mental life of human beings' – a life that, to be precise, is 'nothing other than activity'[36] – 'nature is linked to itself'.[37] It is the identity of the essence of the productive activity of humans and of the productive activity of nature that is underlined, in the sense that the 'essence' of human beings, which is to say their 'vital activity',[38] is nothing other than a part of the vital productive activity of nature. Conceived as naturally and objectively productive, human beings appear as parts of the objective power of nature itself, as vital degrees of intensity of that which is in itself this productive power which affirms itself as a part of the totality of nature.

As with the ontology of relation that precedes it, this ontology of action – which conceives of human activity as part of the natural productive activity that affirms itself in actuality in a precise and determined making – is also at the heart of the apparatus critical of any philosophy of subjectivity. Here, nature is not conceived of as a subject of power that is affirmed in the activity of human beings. Nature is conceived in exactly the same manner as Proposition 18 in Part I of *Ethics* conceives God: as 'the immanent, not the transitive cause of all things'.[39] Which means nothing other than that God is not an agent-subject which, having engendered reality according to its own ends, governs it from outside: 'Everything that is, is in God',[40] which is to say that everything is in nature in such a way that nature acts by producing only itself, it produces nothing external to it, and thus nothing is conceivable outside of it. Nature is immanent rather than exterior to its proper productive activity, and therefore cannot be a subject: in Spinozist

used it with respect to Marx in his study *L'ontologie de Marx*; see in particular Part I, chapter 3 and Part II, chapter 3).
[36] Marx, *Early Writings*, 327.
[37] Ibid., 328.
[38] Ibid.
[39] Spinoza, *Ethics* I, 18; *CWS* I, 428.
[40] Spinoza, *Ethics* I, 18 Dem.; *CWS* I, 428.

terms, *natura naturans* (productive nature) is identical to *natura naturata* (nature produced).

Marx's point of departure is the conception of human beings as part of the productive power of nature, as constitutively dependent on the activity of nature that is affirmed each time and with all of them. Hence the object of his investigation can only be that which determines what apparatuses and what conditions have made it so that the majority of human beings live and conceive of themselves as separate from this power which engenders and determines them. The defining factor of history is that a certain number of historical and social apparatuses of domination have made it so that the natural productive power that is affirmed in the activity and relations between human beings is turned against them, that this power is only affirmed to their detriment, that it is affirmed only in weakening them, and that it is deployed as a means to reduce them to powerlessness. At the heart of this turning of the productive power of nature against human beings, who cannot be understood as anything other than parts of this same power, there is labour, or, more precisely, the becoming-labour of production or the imposition on production of the labour form. From the *1844 Manuscripts* onwards, the question for Marx is to determine what becomes of 'the *act of production* within *labour*',[41] or, more to the point, to comprehend under what causes and conditions the act of production could be liberated, freed from labour. Marx writes that:

> the relationship of labour to the act of production *within labour* . . . is the relationship of the worker to his own activity as something which is alien and does not belong to him, activity as passivity, power as impotence, procreation as emasculation, the worker's own physical and mental energy, his personal life . . . as an activity directed against himself, which is independent of him and does not belong to him.[42]

The same terms are used in *The German Ideology* to describe the reversal of natural power into social impotence, activity into passivity: 'Labour, the only connection which still links [human beings] with the productive forces and with their own existence, has lost all semblance of self-activity and only sustains their life by stunting it.'[43] In labour, human beings experience their own lack of power, the proof of their separation from their own capacity to

---

[41] Marx, *Early Writings*, 327 (Marx's emphasis).
[42] Ibid. (emphasis added).
[43] Marx and Engels, *The German Ideology*, 96.

act: the appearance of labour as a 'negative form of self-activity'[44] is determined by their separation from the forces of production, reducing every individual to their own force, expressed in the practical relationships between individuals. This separation finds its source in private property: productive forces are no longer those of individuals – who combine their own practical or productive potential in deploying them – but those of private property, that is to say of individuals insofar as they are proprietors, which means in competition and opposition, in the experience of non-relation. As forces of private property, the productive forces begin to carry out an autonomous existence, independent of the individuals themselves and their actual productive relationships. Thus dispossessed of their own productive power, individuals are 'robbed . . . of all real life content' and become 'abstract individuals',[45] or exactly what Marx in his later texts calls 'pure subjects' – owners of only an abstract force of labour. The fact that these abstract individuals find in work the verification of their impotence and the negation of their power of activity – their becoming the pure subjects of an abstract labour power is indicated when Marx and Engels write that the productive forces become attached only to private individual proprietors who 'have taken the figure of things' (*eine sachliche Gestalt angenomen haben*)[46] – signifies that the productive forces appear, under the regime of private property, as 'things' that are means of production, from which those proprietors who are simple owners of labour power are precisely excluded. This is what leads to a relation between abstract subjectivity and the productive activity detached from it, accumulated and reified in the form of means of production, which the former does not have direct access to.

To put this in the terms used by Marx in his maturity, the condition of the transformation of money into capital is the exchange of money for 'the power of living labour', that is to say, for a commodity that has the particular quality that its use and consumption make possible the increase of exchange value. However, it is necessary to add that the condition of the transformation of money into capital and the possessor of money into a capitalist is that 'free workers . . . will be found available within the sphere of circulation, on the market'.[47] The capitalist does not create the 'free worker' but finds him already there among the human beings who have nothing to sell but their labour, a commodity that is ready and compelled to be sold because of the

---

[44] Ibid.
[45] Ibid.
[46] Ibid. Translation modified.
[47] Marx, *Economic Manuscripts of 1861–1863*, 37.

separation from the means of subsistence, searching for a buyer, which is to say an owner of money that becomes a capitalist in the buying of labour power. The condition of this 'free worker' is 'the absence of the objective conditions for the realization of his or her labour capacity'.[48] This state of 'freedom' in regard to the objective conditions (object of labour and means of labour) through which it would put to work its potential to work, makes the free worker, the possessor of labour power, a pure subject separated from all objectivity, 'as a mere subject, a mere personification of his own labour capacity, is a worker'.[49] The free worker, as labourer, is nothing other than the personification of a pure subjective quality, and the individual is nothing more than a living producer and productive being, valid only insofar as it embodies and personifies this subjective quality which is the capacity to work, on the express condition that there is a buyer for this capacity, an owner of the objective conditions of work capable of consuming it.

How to interpret this mode of being of labour power insofar as it is only 'the possibility of labour, available and confined within the living body of the worker, a possibility which is . . . utterly separated from all the objective conditions of its realisation, hence from its own reality'?[50] From what is the subject of labour power 'utterly separated' if not from the conditions of the activation of its power as an effective power and therefore as its own active and effective being? Marx also recognises here that 'effective labour' is the productive activity of human beings insofar as they are living beings (or 'beings of needs') producing the means of their own life: 'Since actual labour is the appropriation of nature for the satisfaction of human needs, the activity through which the metabolism (*Stoffwechsel*) between man and nature is mediated, to denude labour capacity of the means of labour, the objective conditions for the appropriation of nature through labour, is to denude it, also, of the means of life.'[51] The impotence of the subject as a simple possessor of labour power is such that, separated from the objective conditions of putting to work its own productive activity, it is also separated from its own means of subsistence: the 'worker', that is to say, the subject 'freed' from objectivity, is separated from the most fundamental power of every being with needs, namely the power expressed and affirmed in its activity of procuring the means of subsistence that permit the reproduction of its life. As a disobjectified being, the subject of labour power is no longer capable of

[48] Ibid., 36.
[49] Ibid.
[50] Ibid., 40.
[51] Ibid., 41.

this affirmation of its elementary power to act by which a living being passes from a passively experienced need to the activity of its satisfaction. This is the radical lack of power that Marx qualifies as 'absolute poverty':

> Labour capacity denuded of the means of labour and the means of life is therefore absolute poverty as such, and the worker, as the mere personification of the labour capacity, has his needs in actuality, whereas the activity of satisfying them is only possessed by him as a non-objective capacity (a possibility) confined within his own subjectivity.[52]

The power of the subject to act is only a purely interior or internal possibility that the subject is incapable of activating by itself to the extent that the objective conditions for externalising it are the property of another: its own power to act is therefore separated from it, made to face it in the objective form of labour or value personified by the capitalist who is capable of buying labour power, by the consumer of this commodity which has as its use value the creation of value, the valorisation of exchange value.

Marx never ceases to be to attentive to the modifications productive activity undergoes when it takes the form of labour: the entry of production into 'the interior of labour' is certainly not a new phenomenon; it is on the contrary an immemorial process that begins with the first forms of the division of labour. But modern capitalist society has given this process a considerable amplification, one without precedent and that leads to its completion. This is why there should be no mistake about the prospect of a 'suppression of work' (which is also that of a 'surpassing' – *Aufhebung* – of labour[53]) in relation to which Marx and Engels situate *The German Ideology*: it is the prospect of the exit of production from the labour form, of an emancipation of production with respect to labour, and obviously not

---

[52] Ibid.
[53] On this point, see Marx and Engels, *The German Ideology*, 88: 'the proletarians, if they are to assert themselves as individuals, have to surpass [*aufheben*] the hitherto prevailing condition of their existence (which has, moreover, been that of all society up to now), namely, labour'. Since for Marx, as for Hegel, *Aufhebung* does not have only the strictly negative sense of suppression or abolition, we have modified the translation and adopted Olivier Tinland's proposal (in *Maîtrise et servitude*, 65–7) to translate *aufheben* by 'surpasser'. What would it mean to abolish or suppress labour if, as Marx says, it has been the condition of the existence of every society up until now? It would not be a matter of suppressing labour purely and simply (that is to say abstractly), but of realising labour as a productive activity that surmounts and surpasses the labour form it has taken in 'every society up to now'.

of finishing with production or productive activity itself – which would be definitively impossible for all natural beings who, like human beings, affirm themselves in their productive activity. The problem for Marx is to determine under what conditions the productive activity of human beings could be expressed in a form that up until now no society has permitted: that of the self-activation of their nature, the individual and collective affirmation of their capacity to act, an affirmation that Spinoza calls 'joyous' and that Marx describes as 'enjoyment'.[54] How to dispense with the social conditions that have – under different forms, but never more intensely than now[55] – always turned the productive activity of human beings against them, thus transforming that which should be elemental in the increase of their power, of their affirmation, and their enrichment and enjoyment, into impotence, negation, passivity, poverty and pain for the majority of human beings?

On this point also *The German Ideology* opens up lines of inquiry that will be taken up in the later works of Marx. The point of departure is that, today, production, or the 'engendering' (*Erzeugung*) of material life, and self-activity (*Selbstbetätigung*) fall outside of each other or 'are separated' (*fallen auseinander*).[56] This too is a result of the becoming-labour of production, which is to say of the separation between producing subjects and their own productive forces which are now externalised and objectified in the form of instruments or means of production that belong to others. The problem and the task is thus to reunite what has been separated, to create a new situation in which 'self-activity coincides with material life', a situation that

---

[54] For Marx, the reduction or saving of labour time is an essential condition for this enjoyment. Thus he notes in the *Grundrisse*: 'Real economy – saving – consists of the saving of labour time . . . but this saving [is] identical with [the] development of the productive force. Hence in no way [is it] abstinence from enjoyment, but rather the development of power, of capabilities of production, and hence both of the capabilities as well as the means of consumption. The capability to enjoy is a condition of consumption, hence its primary means, and this capability is the development of an individual potential, a force of production' (*Grundrisse*, 711. Translation modified).

[55] It is true that the reduction of human beings to impotence has previously taken forms more violent and atrocious than those of today (notably in ancient slavery and feudal servitude). (With respect to the manner in which 'the civilized horrors of overwork are grafted onto the barbaric horrors of slavery, serfdom, etc.', such as in the cotton fields of the American South, see *Capital, Volume I*, 345.) Nonetheless, the reduction to impotence has never been greater in the sense that it is now combined with the objective conditions that would permit human beings to collectively deploy the greatest possible power.

[56] Marx and Engels, *The German Ideology*, 96.

produces 'a transformation (*die Verwandlung*) of labour into self-activity'.[57] In *The German Ideology*, before the revolution of 1848 and its failure, Marx seems to think that these elements will be reunited relatively quicky in the radical transformation of the impending situation. The situation has 'now come to such a point that the individuals must appropriate the existing totality of productive forces, not only to achieve self-activity, but, also, merely to safeguard their very existence'.[58] The unprecedented development of the productive forces in and through the universalisation of productive relations, that is to say, through the extension of productive exchanges to a global scale, is accompanied by and engenders a mass of individuals totally dispossessed, reduced to the labour form of production, condemned to labour power and 'totally excluded from any self-activity', reduced to almost total impotence and radically separated from their own activity, at the same moment that this power becomes part of the same planetary extension of the forces and relations of production. It is from this mass of 'proletarians of the present' that Marx expects the radical transformation of the situation: they are forced to bring about this transformation to the extent that their impotence has reached the point that it is now their very existence that is in question. This is a vital reaction for beings whose work reaches the point where it tends to purely and simply annihilate life. Those closest to radical annihilation are also those for whom there is no way out other than through a total and absolute affirmation of themselves.

Marx and Engels here return to points that were central to Marx's texts from 1843 and 1844: 'Only the proletarians of the present day, who are completely shut off from all self-activity, are in a position to achieve a complete and no longer restricted self-activity, which consists in the appropriation of a totality of productive forces and in the development of a totality of capacities entailed by this.'[59] One can almost read here a version of the famous passage from the 'Introduction to the Critique of Hegel's Philosophy of Right', where, in answer to the question of the conditions of emancipation, Marx responds that we find 'in the formation of a class with radical chains ... a sphere which has a universal character because of its universal suffering ... which is, in a word, the total loss of humanity and which can therefore redeem itself only through the total redemption of humanity'.[60] But in relation to this text, first published in the *Deutsche-Französische Jahrbücher*, *The*

---

[57] Ibid., 97.
[58] Ibid., 96.
[59] Ibid.
[60] Marx, *The Early Writings*, 256.

German Ideology introduces a new emphasis: the theme of emancipation is placed in relation with the state of the productive forces and the relations of production or modes of exchange. This new analysis makes it possible to understand that if the proletarians of the present are the ones to institute total self-activity, this is not because they are now absolutely excluded from all self-activity;[61] rather, it is primarily due to the current development of the productive forces, to what the instruments of production and exchange have undergone: not just in terms of the restrictions of commerce (*Verkehr*), but at the same time in terms of the global extension of 'the instruments of production' to human society itself, since this makes it possible to identify production with the totality of relations between human beings. From now on it is no longer a limited part of society that is productive, but the whole of society, and this society knows itself to not be limited since it is extended to the whole world. There is no longer a difference between society and production: society is entirely productive, every relation or human exchange is now immediately or mediately productive. Human beings are nothing other than their relations, and these relations are universally productive; there is nothing human that is not productive. It this situation, in its radical historical novelty, that opens up the possibility of a total self-activation of humanity.

This is the accomplishment of capitalism:[62] rendering society totally productive, according to the precise sense that capitalism has given production, as no longer just an activity that engenders use values, but an activity producing surplus value through the exploitation of labour power. *The German Ideology* gives us a glimpse of what is at stake in the total appropriation by the proletariat of this totality of productive forces, of the instruments of production and the relations of production of an actual society insofar as it is a totality oriented towards and by production. In one and the same act, such an appropriation suppresses the specifically capitalist form of production while conserving the content of a totally productive society, the unlimited character of the forces and productive exchanges that constitute the space of a total and multiform power of human beings, which is their complete self-activation: 'Only at this stage does self-activity coincide with material life, which corresponds to the development of individuals into complete individuals and the casting-off of all natural limitations.'[63]

---

[61] According to a reversal that would be purely speculative and therefore Hegelian.

[62] As a variation of this, it is also clear in our eyes that this is what Soviet 'communism' accomplished.

[63] Marx and Engels, *The German Ideology*, 97.

CONCLUSION 129

This passage from *The German Ideology* can immediately be put in relation with another, later passage, from the *Grundrisse*:

Capital's ceaseless striving towards the general form of wealth drives labour beyond the limits of its natural paltriness and thus creates the material elements for the development of the rich individuality which is as all-sided in its production as in its consumption, and whose labour also therefore appears no longer as labour, but as the full development of activity itself, in which natural necessity in its direct form has disappeared; because a historically created need has taken the place of the natural one.[64]

Beyond the theme of the appropriation of the totality of productive forces by the proletariat (who no longer appear in the passage from the *Grundrisse*), the key point to note, according to the terms of the *Grundrisse*, is that 'capital is productive, i.e. an essential relation for the development of the social productive forces'.[65] Here we find that it is the becoming totally productive of human society under capitalism that is the issue: that the surpassing of capitalism depends not on the contradictions that develop in its interior, or on the negation of its own immanent negativity, but on a total realisation of the positive tendency of the becoming productive of society that animates it and which it accomplishes. It is this same specifically capitalist character of production (thanks to exploitation, surplus labour, or surplus value, and not the production of use values) that takes on here, in Marx's eyes, an eminently positive characteristic: 'the great historic quality of capital is to create this surplus labour, superfluous labour from the standpoint of mere use value, mere subsistence'.[66] In other words, it is the development without limits of surplus labour ('surplus labour above and beyond necessity has itself become a general need arising out of individual needs'[67]) that has for its consequence the always increasing reduction of necessary labour: thus one arrives at a situation where 'the productive powers of labour, which capital incessantly whips onward with its unlimited mania for wealth ... have flourished to the stage where the possession and preservation of general wealth require a lesser labour time of society as a whole'.[68]

[64] Marx, *Grundrisse*, 325.
[65] Ibid.
[66] Ibid.
[67] Ibid.
[68] Ibid.

It is from this point on that the reversal can operate: the development without restriction of surplus labour leads to a totally productive social form, in which there is no human activity that is not productive in the capitalist sense of the term, that is to say, whose surplus value cannot be extracted; but this totally productive society is also such that there is an immense disproportion between necessary labour and the product of labour. The effect of production, its product, no longer has a common measure with the necessary labour and the average time necessary to produce it:

> to the degree that large industry develops, the creation of real wealth comes to depend less on labour time and on the amount of labour employed than on the power of the agencies set in motion during labour time, [which is] . . . out of all proportion to the direct labour time spent on their production, but depends rather on the general state of science and on the progress of technology, or the application of this science to production.[69]

The development of the forces of production is such that it is also an extension of their intensity; 'hence where labour in which a human being does what a thing could do has ceased',[70] society is on the path of accumulating machines and technology; that is to say, the application of science to production produces greater effects than one can hope to obtain from the consummation of human labour power. 'The theft of alien labour time, on which the present wealth is based, appears a miserable foundation in the face of this new one, created by large-scale industry itself.'[71] It thus appears that 'real wealth' has nothing to do with wealth as it currently exists: 'Real wealth manifests itself . . . in the monstrous disproportion between the labour time applied, and its product, as well as in the qualitative imbalance between labour, reduced to a pure abstraction, and the power of the production process it superintends.'[72]

It is thus the place and the role of human beings in the process of production which eventually changes overall. The *things* (which is to say machines) take the place of human beings in terms of what they are capable of producing; we are witnessing an objectivation of production, the detachment of production from the expenditure and consumption of subjective activity,

[69] Ibid., 704.
[70] Ibid., 325.
[71] Ibid., 705.
[72] Ibid.

from a subjective capacity to work; work becomes more and more an activity of the control of production by things and through things: 'Labour no longer appears so much to be included within the production process; rather, the human being comes to relate more as watchman and regulator to the production process itself.'[73] In these conditions necessary labour is reduced to a miserable residue: 'The surplus labour of the mass has ceased to be the condition for the development of general wealth, just as the non-labour of the few, for the development of the general powers of the human head.'[74] This drastic reduction of necessary labour could perhaps only engender a crisis of capitalism, insofar as the latter subsists only on the express condition of making necessary labour the condition of possibility of the extortion of surplus labour. In the context of this reduction of the mass of necessary labour thanks to mechanisation, it follows that the revolutionary struggle consists in the appropriation by workers of their own surplus labour, that is to say, the transformation of 'available time' into 'free time' – into time available for the free formation of human beings, for the increase of their collective and individual power, for the intensification and extension of their life: 'the free development of individualities, and hence not the reduction of necessary labour time as to posit surplus labour, but rather the general reduction of the necessary labour of society to a minimum, which then corresponds to the artistic, scientific etc. development of the individuals in the time set free, and with the means created, for all of them'.[75] The revolutionary appropriation of surplus labour as free time and available time transforms human beings, in the sense their power to act and play is radically augmented: 'Free time – which is both idle time and time for higher activity – has naturally transformed its possessor into a different subject, and he then enters into the direct production process as this different subject.'[76] This results in the unprecedented development of the productive forces, 'the liberation of social industriousness',[77] which makes it possible to pass from capitalism, as an economy of rarity and misery, to communism (its overcoming in a 'higher form'[78]) as an economy of abundance, of riches and enjoyment: 'The saving of labour time [is] equal to an increase of free time, i.e. time for the full development of the individual, which in turn reacts back upon the productive

[73] Ibid.
[74] Ibid.
[75] Ibid., 706.
[76] Ibid., 712.
[77] Negri, *Marx Beyond Marx*, 147.
[78] Marx, *Grundrisse*, 712.

power of labour as itself the greatest productive power.'[79] It can no longer be said that the productivity of human beings is the same as their productive labour, since it is precisely the elimination of the latter which makes it possible for human beings to develop and deploy their own unheard-of human productivity in its relation with their own particular human enjoyment:[80] the 'ability to enjoy', Marx writes, is the condition of consumption and 'its primary means'.[81] The condition of the 'capacity to enjoy' is itself the same as the 'reduction of labour time', that is to say, the reduction of necessary labour and the revolutionary appropriation of time consecrated to surplus labour by its transformation into free time utilised for the increase of the power to act and play.

Detaching production from the *subjective* power of labour, placing it entirely in the objective machinery of things, is to engender the 'social individual' who no longer belongs to the masses who toil away, nor to the few who understand, but to society itself insofar as it controls and regulates its production by means of a knowledge of the natural processes which permit it to be 'transformed into an industrial process'. It is therefore the development of productive forces under the form of 'large-scale industry' that Marx expects to bring about the transfer of production from the *subjective power* of human beings to the *objective forces* of things, insofar as these forces are mastered and controlled by human beings. But this transformation or mutation would at the same time entail that 'production based on exchange value breaks down',[82] that is to say, the collapse of capitalism itself, as the production that it implements aims to generate surplus value by exploiting labour power considered as the specific commodity, available on the market, the use value of which makes possible an increase in the exchange value.

It is therefore the same development of productive forces that leads to a stage which appears to be clearly 'miserable', as Marx says of the specifically capitalist production of wealth founded upon the exploitation of labour power: this basis for the production of wealth, at a certain stage (which we have not yet reached today) of capitalist production, finally appears as too

---

[79] Ibid., 711.
[80] The glorification of productive labour, such as it was put to work in Soviet communism, would thus be in direct contradiction with the thought of Marx.
[81] Ibid. [Translators note: in the English translation the references to enjoyment are obscured by the translation of 'Die Fähigkeit des Genusses' as capability to consume. I am following Fischbach's use of the French translation to translate it as capability to enjoy.]
[82] Ibid., 705.

narrow a base; it reveals its own character as a fetter (negative, if one must, but only in the sense that it makes possible an *affirmation* that is still insufficient for social production), and it manifests itself as an economy that is still one of penury and rarity, where a production entirely entrusted to things (to machines), socially regulated and controlled, would make possible the definite and irreversible passage to an economy of abundance. The social production of wealth thus changes its base: no longer resting on the limited, miserable and petty base of the masses of those who only have their labour power to sell, from which capital extorts surplus value, it is transposed to the newly expanded base of all of society. 'In this transformation', Marx writes, 'it is neither the direct human labour [the worker] himself performs, nor the time during which he works, but rather the appropriation of his own general productive power, his understanding of nature and his mastery over it by virtue of his presence as a social body – it is, in a word, the development of the social individual which appears as the great foundation-stone of production and of wealth.'[83]

Here we see the resurgence of the theme of the appropriation of the totality of the productive forces, which appears in *The German Ideology* as the condition for the identification of the production of material life with the self-activity of human beings. In the *Grundrisse* as in *The German Ideology* there is an appropriation by human beings of 'their productive force in general', and therefore an overcoming of the impotence which is the form of their separation with respect to their own productive forces. But the *Grundrisse* adds to this an element that we could qualify as properly Spinozist, namely the idea that such an appropriation of their own potential by human beings presupposes and entails knowledge, specifically the knowledge of nature or of the 'forces of nature'. In order for 'the great foundation-stone of production and of wealth' to no longer involve the exploitation of the masses of subjects as possessors of labour power but rather the 'appropriation [by humanity] of [its] own productive force in general', it is necessary that 'the comprehension and domination of nature' – i.e. the knowledge of things that makes it possible for natural productivity to be transformed into industrial productivity – be placed under the control of associated individuals. The 'social individual' is thus one for whom knowledge of the nature of things and the characteristics of natural productivity is extended into industrial or social productivity, such that 'the human being comes to relate more as watchman and regulator to the production process itself'.

[83] Ibid.

It is uniquely through scientific knowledge as 'general social knowledge'[84] that it is possible to realise the coincidence or the identification of the production of material life and the self-activity of human beings, in the sense that human beings appropriate their collective and individual capacity to act, their human or social power, not only in developing their knowledge of nature, but also in transforming 'knowledge into a direct force of production',[85] thereby becoming the adequate causes of their own capacity to act, insofar as 'the conditions of the process of social life itself have come under the control of the general intellect'.[86] In these conditions the productive forces of society are productive 'under the form of knowledge', but since this knowledge is first a knowledge of nature and of its own productivity, the productive forces are engendered as an articulation of the productive power of nature that they prolong and extend: engendered by the 'general social knowledge', they appear as 'the immediate organs of social practice', but they also augment the power of this practice because they are founded on a knowledge of natural productivity that prolongs and intensifies 'the real life process'.[87]

Several remarks are possible in closing. First, it would appear that today we are very far from the point of view of the identity of material production and human self-activity. What is called 'immaterial production',[88] notably in the form of the production of knowledge permitting the mastery of natural and social productivity, has certainly become a decisive element of capitalist production. But far from this being a source of enthusiasm and cause for

[84] Ibid., 706.
[85] Ibid.
[86] Ibid.
[87] The passage from the *Grundrisse* that we are citing goes under the name of the 'Fragment on Machines' and has been the subject of many commentaries (of particular note are Antonio Negri's *Marx beyond Marx*; Lucien Sève's 'La question du communism' and *Penser avec Marx aujourd'hui*; and André Gorz's *The Immaterial*). These rest generally on the idea (which we take up in our account) that this text of Marx describes a possible evolution of capitalism towards a situation that one might think has something to do with our present and our reality. However, considering that *Capital* corrects, rectifies and amends numerous points of the prior analysis in the *Grundrisse*, Jacques Bidet warns against drawing hasty conclusions from the 'Fragment on Machines' (see his *Théorie Générale*, 463, and *Explication et reconstruction du Capital*, 117–21).
[88] Michael Hardt and Antonio Negri clarify that 'material production ... creates the means of social life' while 'immaterial production, [as] the production of ideas, images, knowledges, communication, cooperation, and affective relations, tends to create not the means of social life but social life itself. Immaterial production is biopolitical.' Hardt and Negri, *Multitude*, 146.

general celebration,[89] it is important not to forget that the actual production of wealth rests always primarily on the miserable base of the exploitation of the labour of the vast majority of humanity. It is only in the globally central zones that we see production resting less and less on the surplus of the masses and more and more on the control of the objective process, a control itself immediately dependent on the scientific mastery of the productivity of natural and social life; moreover, this is always realised at the cost of the extortion of surplus value from the mass of workers in the peripheral zones of the global economic system.

On the strictly philosophical level, this leads us to think that Heidegger was certainly not wrong to consider the era of total production to be still far from complete, that we have not yet reached the ultimate stage. But it remains certain that this apparent accord between Heidegger and Marx cannot conceal a profound misunderstanding: just as much as that of Spinoza, the thought of Marx cannot be understood at the level of a final and decisive accomplishment of the metaphysics of subjectivity in the metaphysics in production. What Heidegger calls 'production' or 'the productive comportment of Dasein' relates to what Marx calls labour, that is, in Heidegger's terms, to the 'process of the objectivation of the actual (*Vergegenständlichung des Wirklichen*) through man experienced as subjectivity'.[90] But labour is not the activity of production in general but only the form that it takes in capitalism in the opposition between subjective labour power and the objective conditions of labour, where the former is separated from the latter. Marx elaborates a conception of productivity that has this in common with the Spinozist conception of natural productivity: that it justifies a critique of all production reduced to the confrontation of a subject with an object, which is to say, reduced to labour. Heidegger appears not to see that, if this a-subjective conception of productivity supposes a *Vergegenständlichung*, it is

---

[89] Hardt and Negri's enthusiasm is itself somewhat guarded: 'We do not mean to suggest that the paradigm of immaterial production is some paradise in which we produce freely in common and share equally the common social wealth' (ibid., 149). Nevertheless, the very fact that they have to make this explicit suggests that their way of describing immaterial production could be considered, if not as paradise, then at least as its antechamber. In fact, they do not wait for the salvation of a simple extension of immaterial labour, and they do not claim, since it would be false, that there are now more workers in the category of immaterial labour than material labour; they observe only that the human activities belonging to immaterial labour are for capital today the greatest sources of valorisation and profit, and for this reason they conclude that the struggle must henceforth give priority to the concept of immaterial labour.

[90] Heidegger, 'Letter on Humanism', 220.

not solely that of an objectivation of reality, but first and foremost that of the objectivation of humanity itself, which is to say, humanity considered not as a subject but on the contrary as a thing in nature, as a being existing objectively in nature. Neglecting this *Vergegenständlichung* of humanity, Heidegger is not able to see the fundamental rapprochement of the Marxist and Spinozist positions in terms of their own understanding of the essential finitude of humanity.[91] He does not see that an ontology of natural productivity is a fundamentally critical apparatus with respect to any metaphysics of subjectivity in that it makes possible, with Marx, the understanding that the formation of the modern paradigm of subjectivity is directly dependent on a specific and determinant form of production: that it is connected to a becoming-production of the natural productivity of humanity, then to a becoming-work of this human productivity consisting of the properly capitalist reduction of humanity to the impotence of a pure subjectivity, the simple owner of labour power, separated from the objective conditions of affirmation (individual and collective, natural and social) of its own productive power.

---

[91] This aspect has been particularly emphasised by Jakob Hommes in his books *Zwiespältiges Dasein. Die existentiale Ontologie von Hegel bis Heidegger* and *Der technische Eros*.

Appendix

The Question of Alienation: Frédéric Lordon, Marx and Spinoza[1]

The question of how a return to Marx and Spinoza can make it possible to construct a concept of alienation that would still be relevant for us today is the central question both of this book and also of a major work by Frédéric Lordon, *Capitalisme, désir et Servitude: Marx and Spinoza*, which appeared in 2010 (translated in 2014 as *Willing Slaves of Capital: Spinoza and Marx on Desire*). If there is a terrain common to Lordon's *Spinoza and Marx* and our own *Marx with Spinoza*, it can only be a Spinozist one, and therefore in accord with the idea that alienation must be thought in relation to a regime of activity or acting more than to a certain form of being: that alienation is experienced first in terms of what we do (or what we cannot do), as primarily a restriction on what we can or are able to do, and subsequently as a restriction on what we are or can be.

With its title and subtitle, Lordon's book is placed in relation to a philosophical tradition that has its roots in France, going back at least to Althusser, and that consists in reading Marx and Spinoza together: a tradition which posits that it is Spinoza (not Hegel) who makes it possible to understand Marx, and that it is Marx (more than Descartes) who makes it possible to understand Spinoza. The first approach effectively makes possible a reading of Spinoza by Marx, focused on the traces that remain in the text of Marx, mostly the young Marx, of his reading of Spinoza, notably in his anthropological (human beings as *Teil der Natur* or *pars naturae*) and ontological conceptions (nature as productive totality, human history as a continuation of natural history). The second approach (using Marx to read Spinoza) appears more adventurous and risky, but it can justify itself in terms

---

[1] [Translators note: What follows was originally published on the website La vie des Idées (www.laviedesidées.fr) and later published in the second edition of *La production des hommes: Marx avec Spinoza* (Paris: Vrin, 2014).]

of multiple points of intersection. For example, with Spinoza and Marx, it is a matter of two philosophers who, in the context of the entire western tradition, are rare in terms of their specific claim to be partisans of democracy. That said, Lordon's book is not the work of a historian of philosophy, and the reader should not expect an internally detailed reading of either Marx or Spinoza (nonetheless, someone completely ignorant of Spinoza will learn things from Lordon's book). This is not a critique on my part, nor is it a reservation: it is a matter only of saying that Lordon does not study the thought of Spinoza or of Marx, or their relation, for themselves. His aim is rather to make possible an understanding of the transformation that capitalism has undergone in the last twenty-five or thirty years, and that it is still undergoing now. Marx and Spinoza are invoked here insofar as they facilitate this understanding. One can, however, note that Lordon's reference to Spinoza is noticeably more extensive than his reference to Marx, and that Spinozist language and concepts (beginning with such technical concepts such as affect, affection, conatus and power) make more of a contribution to his book than do properly Marxist concepts.

But this apparent imbalance is somewhat misleading insofar as the framework of Lordon's reflection on capitalism is in reality directly borrowed from Marx: very rightly, he starts from the idea that what is ultimately central to capitalism, and what it has itself invented, is wage labour or salaried work. This is to some extent a major thesis in Marx: in all the modes of production and social formations anterior to capitalism, the structures of domination were constituted outside of labour, or they commanded labour from the outside. In capitalism, however, the social relation of domination is interior and immanent to labour. It is the social form taken by labour which in itself engenders the social relation of domination. This has the notable consequence that, while in the non-capitalist social formations the relations of domination are manifest, in capitalism they are obscured. Or, more to the point, the relations of domination in capitalism appear as something other than they are: they do not appear as relations of domination, but take the form of relations that are not imposed, not forced, that are freely consented to and freely chosen. It is thus that the relation between labour and capital appears as a relation of exchange between two partners equally free and autonomous, who are in agreement on the price for which the one freely accepts to sell to the other the commodity which it possesses, namely its capacity for work or labour power. This appearance of an entirely equitable exchange (work for a salary) between two equally free individuals is understood by Marx to be a real appearance: it is not only that things present themselves as such, they actually function this way. However, this is not because the appearance corresponds to what it is because of what is true; on the contrary, it is the reality itself that is false, and the appearance only corresponds to this mystification.

The objective of Lordon's book is to understand how this mystification can function, and it is in terms of arriving at this objective that he draws on the conceptual vocabulary forged by Spinoza: it is a matter of 'reexamining' the problem of salary 'through the passions',[2] that is to say, of thinking 'at the intersection of the Spinozist theory of passions and the Marxist theory of wage-labour'.[3] But it is necessary first of all to challenge the first answer that would present itself, that of what could be called 'voluntary servitude'. This answer would be as follows: the worker knows very well that, in exchanging the use of their labour power for a salary, they have already given themselves over hand and foot to capital to the extent that, in accepting the exchange and its terms, they have in reality already accepted that the labour they sell is effectively no longer their own. The worker would understand all of this perfectly well, would be fully conscious of this fact, but accepts this when it submits to these conditions voluntary, understanding that its own activity is no longer its own, and that it is instead placed entirely in the service of the self-valorisation of capital through the usage it makes of this activity.

On this point Lordon is very clear: this 'explanation' is nothing of the sort. And he sees equally clearly that it is Spinoza and Marx who make it possible to overcome it. If Marx and Spinoza are in agreement in challenging this explanation, it is because it rests entirely on a metaphysics of subjectivity that they have both radically broken with. Lordon begins, then, by arguing that voluntary servitude does not explain anything. One of two things must be true: either the servitude is truly servitude, and thus one can only suffer it, which means that one can neither choose to accept it nor choose to reject it; or the servitude is truly voluntary, which means that having accepted it one could also change it, and thus it is not truly servitude. The incommensurable difficulties inherent in this 'concept' of voluntary servitude come from the concept of the subject or subjectivity upon which it rests. Given a subject, and a truth, that is to say, a subject that knows what it does and why it does it, one is confronted with the embarrassment of the following situations: 'he follows a guru but nobody forced him to; she wears the veil but it was her decision; he/she shuts him/herself away in the office for twelve hours a day, but purely out of personal choice, uncompelled by anyone . . .'.[4] Faced

---

[2] Lordon, *Willing Slaves of Capital*, xi. Translation modified.
[3] Ibid., xiii.
[4] Ibid., 54.

with cases of this type, one can protest in essentially one of two ways: either these are cases that no subject worthy of the same could truly consent to; or they are cases in which the consent of these subjects has been fraudulently obtained. In the first instance, it is necessary to know why these particular subjects consent all the same, which leads without fail to the second instance (of consent fraudulently obtained); but then it would be necessary to explain how it is that the subject – which, by hypothesis, knows what it does and why it does it – can be so easily fooled and misled. 'But does not then the fact of such intermittent lapses call into question their very quality as subjects?'[5]

One can only truly escape these difficulties and aporias by renouncing the fiction of the autonomous subject, sovereign and endowed with an interior life, which would then lead to challenging any opposition between exterior constraint and free and internal consent. The alternative between constraint and consent is false because in reality there is nothing other than external constraint: it is in the nature of finite modes that we are determined and acted upon by external constraints. The external constraint comes first and it is the rule: the one who consents is no less determined than the one who is constrained. The one who consents, and who believes that they consent freely, is in reality determined to consent. He or she believes that they move themselves, when, like everything else in the world, they are moved and put into movement by something other than themselves. But they will be more inclined to ignore the fact that they are moved by something else when this external cause engenders joyous affects in them: 'the forgetting of exo-determination . . . is even deeper when the causes that are ignored are those of joyful affects'; everything comes to pass as if there is a tendency to 'experience this as their own sovereign wish' that renders joy 'incontestable'.[6]

It might seem that we are here very far from the question of wage labour, but Lordon demonstrates on the contrary that we are right in the middle of it, because it is in wage labour that we find an apparatus that produces consent, and therefore an apparatus that produces joyous determination. A wage labourer is essentially an individual who has been determined to be placed in the service of another, in the service of realising the projects and enterprise of another, but in such a way that they live joyously this enlistment of their power to act in the service of another, which is that of their patron's conatus or their master's desires. For a long time the conatus of the employer has produced these happy workers by managing their access to the

[5] Ibid., 55. Translation modified.
[6] Ibid., 92.

pleasures of consumption. However, the conatus of the neoliberal employer has gone much further: it is no longer content to produce the workers' joy on the transitive basis of providing external objects to consume and the means to pay for them (money). Rather, '[t]he strength of the neoliberal form of the employment relation lies precisely in the re-internalisation of the objects of desire, not merely as desire for money but as desire for other things, for new, intransitive satisfactions, satisfactions inherent in the work activities themselves.'[7] It is therefore a matter of the desire of the employer extending into the desire of the worker in order to produce joyous affects in it directly: it is 'an attempt to exercise control in a manner so profound, so complete', that it cannot be accomplished without 'the complete surrender of "interiority"', without the 'total possession of individuals', without 'subordinating the entire life and being of employees' and effecting 'a complete capture of their power to act'.[8] It is a question of the employees being completely invaded by the enterprise, which arrives at this result by producing directly 'in them' the joyful affects that will guarantee their total participation in the enterprise, which is to say, their complete alienation from it.

This is what leads Lordon to completely revise the terms in which it has been possible up to now (notably in the Marxist tradition) to think the relation between wage labour and alienation. Thus far, I can say that I am in complete accord with Lordon on one essential point: namely, that the liberal and neoliberal apparatus rests on the fiction of autonomous subjects who consent by themselves to enter into the salary relation. Thus, it cannot be a question of escaping the alienation of the wage relation by a 'reaffirmation of the sovereign autonomy of the subjects who regain the free command of their lives'. Lordon is entirely right to say of those who adopt such a position that 'there is deep intellectual kinship that binds them to the liberal thought that they imagine themselves fighting'.[9] Lordon goes further, however, since he considers that at its base the concept of alienation becomes useless once one recognises that the fact of external constraint, of being determined by another than oneself, is not an accident that influences otherwise free beings, but rather the fundamental trait of our condition. What is the point of speaking of alienation if one no longer understands it to be the loss of something essential to the subject (its freedom or autonomy) but an unavoidable condition (such as passionate servitude) from which no human being can initially escape? Alienation is thus at its foundation nothing other

---

[7] Ibid., 60.
[8] Ibid., 79–80.
[9] Ibid., 135.

than 'another word for heterodetermination, namely for passionate servitude, the human condition itself'.[10]

The concept of alienation would at this point be so intimately intertwined with the metaphysics of subjectivity to the point that it would be impossible, in making use of the one, not to reintroduce something of the other. This is the point arrived at by even the best of Spinozists, such as Deleuze, who understands alienation as the condition of an individual being separated from its capacity to act, of being unable to become actual. This sort of escape from alienation – for an individual which still resembles something like a subject – would be the reappropriation of something of itself and the search to coincide with itself, to coincide with its own capacity to act. On this point Lordon is in agreement with Pascal Sévérac, who argues that for Spinoza power cannot be separated from its actualisation: all power, finite or infinite, is at each moment completely actual, is always everything that it can be, without reserve and without possible diversion, therefore without being subject to a loss that would be its 'alienation'. If, then, one continues to use the concept of alienation, it can only be on the condition that one ceases to think of it under the scheme of loss or separation, and instead thinks of it in terms of fixation or limitation; an alienated capacity to act, in this sense, is not a capacity from which the subject is separated or which it would be limited to actualise, it is a capacity in which its effects are limited in number and restricted to one type or form. One could then say that the alienation of a worker occurs when its capacities are limited solely to the sphere of consumption: 'this is what alienation is, not a loss, but closure and contraction'.[11]

An interesting fact, not indicated by Lordon, is that Marx seems to have already had this understanding of alienation in 1844, that is to say, in the period in which his thought is most heavily marked by evidence of his Spinozism. he explains in the *1844 Manuscripts* that human activity takes a great variety of forms and that its alienation consists in its limitation and fixation to one type of activity. But in later works, when conceiving of the separation of the subjective capacity to work from the objective conditions of its actualisation as the condition of possibility of wage labour, he appears to return to a conception of alienation that can be considered subjective. This would seem to be an error: like Spinoza, Marx posits that there is in reality no subject but only hetero-determined individuals. He adds that alienation consists in nothing other than the fact of an individual believing

[10] Ibid., 57.
[11] Ibid., 146.

it is a subject or can be conceived as a subject, and he undertakes to identify and understand what sort of social apparatuses produce subjectivity, or something that can be taken as subject, and how this is engendered as an indispensable condition for the production and reproduction of our social condition. Marx would say therefore that alienation is not something that happens to a subject, rather it consists in the very fact that one thinks of oneself as a subject, and, in this way, is something that is mobilised for the valorisation of capital. However, this process does not alienate a subject which pre-exists it: it produces the subjects which it needs, and it is in being produced as subjects that human beings are alienated individuals.

Beyond a few nuances in the details, one can only admire the way that Lordon demonstrates how Spinoza's thought, at a distance of more than three centuries, can not only continue to be productive in understanding the most pressing issues of our times, but can also continue to open up horizons of liberation.

Bibliography

Althusser, Louis, *For Marx*, trans. Ben Brewster, New York: Verso, 1969.
Althusser, Louis, 'Is It Simple to Be a Marxist in Philosophy?' in *Philosophy and the Spontaneous Philosophy of the Scientists and Other Essays*, trans. Graham Locke, ed. Gregory Elliot, New York: Verso, 1989.
Althusser, Louis, 'Marx in his Limits', in *Philosophy of the Encounter: Later Writings, 1978–1987*, trans. G. M. Goshgarian, ed. François Matheron and Oliver Corpet, New York: Verso, 2014.
Althusser, Louis, *On the Reproduction of Capitalism: Ideology and Ideological State Apparatuses*, trans. G. M. Goshgarian, New York: Verso, 2014.
Althusser, Louis, 'From Capital to Marx's Philosophy', in Louis Althusser and Étienne Balibar, *Reading Capital: The Complete Edition*, trans. Ben Brewster, London: Verso, 2015.
Althusser, Louis, 'The Object of *Capital*', in Louis Althusser and Étienne Balibar, *Reading Capital: The Complete Edition*, trans. Ben Brewster, London: Verso, 2015.
Balibar, Étienne, *Masses, Classes, Ideas: Studies on Politics and Philosophy before and after Marx*, trans. James Swenson, New York: Routledge 1994.
Balibar, Étienne, *The Philosophy of Marx*, trans. Chris Turner, New York: Verso, 1995.
Balibar, Étienne, *La Crainte des Masses: Politique et Philosophie avant et après Marx*, Paris: Galilée, 1997.
Balibar, Étienne, *Spinoza and Politics*, trans. Peter Snowdon, New York: Verso, 1998.
Benussan, Gérard, 'Spinozisme', in *Dictionnaire critique du Marxisme*, Paris: PUF, 1999.
Bidet, Jacques, *Théorie Générale: théorie du droit, de l'économie et de la politique*, Paris: PUF, 1999.

Bidet, Jacques, *Explication et reconstruction du Capital*, Paris: PUF, 2004.
Cassirer, Ernst, 'The Philosophy of History', in *Symbol, Myth, and Culture: Essays and Lectures, 1935–1945*, ed. Donald Philip Verene, New Haven: Yale University Press, 1979.
Deleule, Didier, *Hume et la naissance du libéralisme politique*, Paris: Aubier Montaigne, 1979.
Deleuze, Gilles, *Spinoza: Practical Philosophy*, trans. Robert Hurley, San Francisco: City Lights, 1988.
Deleuze, Gilles, *The Logic of Sense*, trans. Mark Lester with Charles Stivale, New York: Columbia, 1990.
Deleuze, Gilles, *Expressionism in Philosophy: Spinoza*, trans. Martin Joughin, New York: Zone, 1992.
Derrida, Jacques, *Specters of Marx: The State of Debt, The Work of Mourning, and the New International*, trans. Peggy Kamuf, New York: Routledge, 1994.
Derrida, Jacques, 'Marx & Sons', trans. G. Goshgarian, in M. Sprinker ed., *Ghostly Demarcations: A Symposium on Jacques Derrida's Specters of Marx*, New York: Verso, 1999.
Dewey, John, *Art as Experience*, New York: Perigee, 1934.
Estes, Yolanda and Curtis Bowman, eds. *J. G. Fichte and the Atheism Dispute (1798–1800)*, New York: Routledge, 2020.
Feuerbach, Ludwig, *The Fiery Brook: Selected Writings*, trans. Zawar Hanfi, New York: Verso, 2012.
Fischbach, Franck, *L'etre et l'acte*, Paris: Vrin, 2002.
Foucault, Michel, *The Hermeneutics of the Subject: Lectures at the College of France, 1981–1982*, trans. Graham Burchell, ed. Frédéric Gros et al., Picador: New York, 2016.
Gorz, André, *The Immaterial*, trans. Chris Turner, Chicago: Seagull Books, 2010.
Granel, Gerard, 'L'ontologie marxiste de 1844 et la question de la "coupure"', in *Traditions tradition*, Paris: Gallimard, 1972.
Granel, Gerard, 'David Hume, Le cynisme de la production', in *Ecrits Logiques et Politiques*, Paris: Galilée, 1990.
Haarscher, Guy, *L'ontologie de Marx*, Brussels: Editions de L'Université de Bruxelles, 1980.
Hardt, Michael and Antonio Negri, *Multitude: War and Democracy in the Age of Empire*, New York: Penguin, 2004.
Hegel, G. W. F., *Elements of the Philosophy of Right*, trans. H. B. Nisbet, Cambridge: Cambridge University Press, 1991.

Hegel, G. W. F., *The Phenomenology of Spirit*, trans. Terry Pinkard, Cambridge: Cambridge University Press, 2018.
Heidegger, Martin, *Being and Time*, trans. John Macquarrie and Edward Robinson, London: Blackwell, 1962.
Heidegger, Martin, 'Letter on Humanism', in *Basic Writings*, ed. and trans. David Farrell Krell, New York: Harper and Row, 1977.
Heidegger, Martin, *The Basic Problems of Phenomenology*, trans. Alfred Hofstadter, Indianapolis: Indiana University Press, 1982.
Heidegger, Martin, *The History of Beyng*, trans. William McNeil and Jeffrey Powell, Bloomington: Indiana University Press, 2015.
Henry, Michel, *Marx: A Philosophy of Human Reality*, trans. Kathleen McLaughlin, Bloomington: Indiana University Press, 1982.
Hess, Moses, *Berlin, Paris, Londres, La triarche Européene*, trans. Michel Espagne, Tusson: Editions du Lérot, 1988.
Hommes, Jakob, *Zwiespältiges Dasein. Die existentiale Ontologie von Hegel bis Heidegger*, Freiberg: Herder, 1953.
Hommes, Jakob, *Der technische Eros. Das Wesen der materialistischen Geschichtsauffassung*, Freiberg: Herder, 1955.
Kosík, Karel, *Dialectics of the Concrete: A Study of the Problems of Man and World*, Dordrecht: Reidel, 1976.
Lordon, Frédéric, *Willing Slaves of Capital: Spinoza and Marx on Desire*, trans. Gabriel Ash, New York: Verso, 2014. (Originally published as *Capitalisme, désir et servitude: Marx et Spinoza*, Paris: La fabrique Editions, 2010.)
Löwith, Karl, 'The Quest for the Meaning of History', in *Nature, History, and Existentialism and Other Essays on the Philosophy of History*, ed. Arnold Levinson, Evanston: Northwestern University Press, 1966.
Lukács, Georg, *History and Class consciousness: Studies in Marxist Dialectics*, trans. Rodney Livingstone, Cambridge, MA: MIT Press, 1971.
Macherey, Pierre, 'Action et operation: sur la signification éthique du *De Deo*', in *Avec Spinoza*, Paris: PUF, 1992.
Macherey, Pierre, 'Spinoza, the End of History, and the Ruse of Reason', in *In a Materialist Way: Selected Essays*, trans. Ted Stolze, New York: Verso, 1998.
Macherey, Pierre, 'Le Dieu Noir de La Mélancholie', *L'Humanité*, 28 June 2001, at <https://www.humanite.fr/le-dieu-noir-de-la-melancolie-248557>
Macherey, Pierre, *Hegel or Spinoza*, trans. Suzanne Ruddick, Minneapolis: University of Minnesota Press, 2011.
Marx, Karl, 'Letter from Marx to his Father in Trier', 10 November 1937,

at <https://www.marxists.org/archive/marx/works/1837-pre/letters/37_11_10.htm>

Marx, Karl, A Contribution to the Critique of Political Economy, trans. Maurice Dobb, New York: International, 1970.

Marx, Karl, Grundrisse: Foundations of the Critique of Political Economy, trans. M. Nicolaus. New York: Penguin, 1973.

Marx, Karl, 'Critique of the Gotha Program', in The First International and After: Political Writings, trans. David Fernbach, New York: Penguin, 1974.

Marx, Karl, Early Writings, trans. Rodney Livingston and Gregor Benton, New York: Penguin, 1975.

Marx, Karl, Capital, Volume I, trans. Ben Fowkes, New York: Penguin 1977.

Marx, Karl, Economic Manuscripts of 1861–1863, trans. Ben Fowkes, MECW Volume 30, London: Lawrence and Wishart, 1989.

Marx, Karl, 'Notes on Adolph Wagner's "Lehrbuch der politischen Ökonomie" (Second Edition), Volume I, 1879', at <https://www.marxists.org/archive/marx/works/1881/01/wagner.htm>

Marx, Karl and Friedrich Engels, The Holy Family: Or, Critique of Critical Critique, trans. R. Dixon, Moscow: International Publishers, 1956.

Marx, Karl and Friedrich Engels, Gesamtausgabe (MEGA), IV 1, Berlin, Dietz Verlag, 1976.

Marx, Karl and Friedrich Engels, The German Ideology, New York: Prometheus Books, 1998.

Matheron, Alexandre, 'Appendix 1: Interview with Laurent Bove and Pierre François Moreau', in Politics, Ontology, and Knowledge in Spinoza, trans. David Mauzzella and Gil Morejón, ed. Filipo Del, Lucchese, David Maruzzella and Gil Morejón, Edinburgh: Edinburgh University Press, 2020.

Merleau-Ponty, Maurice, Adventures of the Dialectic, trans. Joseph Biens, Evanston: Northwestern University Press, 1973.

Nancy, Jean-Luc, 'Heidegger', in Dictionnaire d'éthique et de philosophie morale, ed. Monique Canto-Sperber, Paris: PUF, 1996.

Negri, Antonio, Marx beyond Marx: Lessons on the Grundrisse, trans. Harry Cleaver et al. New York: Autonomedia, 1991.

Plekhanov, Georgi, The Fundamental Problems of Marxism. Selected Philosophical Works, Volume 3, Moscow: Progress Publishers: Moscow, 1976, at <https://www.marxists.org/archive/plekhanov/1907/fundamentalproblems.htm>

Schmidt, Alfred, The Concept of Nature in Marx, trans. Ben Fowkes, New York: Verso, 1972.

Servois, Julien, 'Etude sur le travail aliéné dans le Manuscrits de 1844 de Marx', Kairos, no. 24, 2004.

Sève, Lucien, Penser avec Marx aujourd'hui. I. Marx et nous, Paris: La Dispute, 2004.

Sève, Lucien, 'La question du communism', at <http://jean-leveque.fr/question-ducommunisme.htm>

Spinoza, Baruch, Ethics, in The Collected Works of Spinoza, Volume I, ed. and trans. Edwin Curley, Princeton: Princeton University Press, 1994.

Spinoza, Baruch, Political Treatise, in The Collected Works of Spinoza, Volume II, ed. and trans. Edwin Curley, Princeton: Princeton University Press, 2016.

Tinland, Olivier, Maîtrise et servitude: Phenoménology de l'esprit, Paris: Ellipses, 2003.

Tosel, André, 'Qu'est-ce qu'agir pour un mode fini selon Spinoza?', Philosophie, no. 53, March 1997.

Tosel, André, 'Des usages "Marxistes" de Spinoza: Leçon de méthode', in Spinoza au XIX Siècle, ed. André Tosel, Paris: Editions de la Sorbonne, 2008.

Vaysse, Jean-Marie, Totalité et subjectivité: Spinoza dans l'idéalisme allemend, Paris: Vrin, 1994.

Vaysse, Jean-Marie, L'inconscient des modernes: Essai sur l'origine métaphysique de la psychanalyse, Paris: Gallimard, 1999.

Vaysse, Jean-Marie Totalité et Finitude: Heidegger et Spinoza, Paris: Vrin, 2004.

Zac, Sylvain, 'Jacobi critique de Spinoza', in Spinoza nel 350th Anniversario della nascita, a cura di Emilia Giancotti, Napoli: Bibliopolis, 1985.

Zac, Sylvain, 'La renaissance de Spinoza dans la philosophie religieuse en Allemagne à l'époque de Goethe', in Essais Spinozistes, Paris: Vrin, 1985.

Zac, Sylvain, Spinoza en Allemagne. Mendelssohn, Lessing et Jacobi, Paris: Méridiens Klincksieck, 1989.

Index

Affects 28, 30–3, 71–4, 140–1
Alienation 4–6, 34, 45–6, 79, 92, 137, 141–3
Althusser, Louis, 1, 7, 14–19, 22, 34, 81, 137
Aristotle, 9, 76

Balibar, Etienne, 5, 15, 38, 70, 120

Capitalism, x, 3, 4, 6, 57, 83, 90, 114, 128, 129, 131, 132, 134n87, 135, 138
Conatus, 31, 102, 138, 140

Deleuze, Gilles, 33, 57, 76, 105n14, 110, 142
Dewey, John, viii

Exploitation, 84n19, 128, 129, 130, 132, 133

Feuerbach, Ludwig, 5, 5n10, 15, 16, 22, 24, 37, 48, 52, 72, 76–7, 108
Foucault, Michel, 11

Granel, Gerard, 5n12, 101n4, 106–7

Hardt, Michael and Negri, Antonio, 99, 134n88, 135n89
Heidegger, Martin, vii–ix, 8, 19, 80, 110–16, 135
Hegel, G.W.F., 4, 5n10, 9, 9n19, 13–14, 17–18, 33–4, 42n22, 45, 66, 90

Henry, Michel, 2n4, 47n40
History, 3–4, 20, 25, 33, 36–40, 51–6, 69, 75, 94, 111, 122, 137

Ideology, 18, 19, 81
Imaginary, 11, 30, 52, 63, 64, 69

Kosík, Karl 56–7

Labour, ix, x, 5, 29, 40, 41, 44, 44n30, 48, 52, 54, 55, 82, 84, 85, 92, 93, 94, 95, 98, 99, 105, 123,132, 135, 138
  Abstract, 70, 86, 87, 87n32, 88, 89, 97, 123, 124, 125
  Concrete, 41, 84, 86, 95, 96, 128
Labour power, 12, 23, 70, 83, 84n19, 85, 87–90, 95–9, 123–5, 127, 130, 132, 135, 138, 139; see also Work
Lordon, Frédéric, 137–43
Löwith, Karl, 36–9, 55

Macherey, Pierre, 1, 13, 15, 19n32, 103n9
Merleau-Ponty, Maurice, 3–5, 7
Marx, Karl,
  Economic and Philosophical Manuscripts of 1844, 5n12, 6, 10, 17, 22, 24, 29, 36, 40, 41, 43, 44, 48, 51, 53, 54, 58, 73, 75, 79, 92, 96, 101, 106, 107, 108, 122, 142
  "Theses on Feuerbach", 25, 53, 99, 102, 119

Marx, Karl (cont.)
  Contribution to the Critique of Political Economy, 55, 61n3, 64–6
  The Grundrisse, 25, 29, 51n18, 81, 82n11, 86, 88, 89, 90, 95, 99, 126n54, 129, 131, 133, 134n87
  Capital: A Critique of Political Economy, Volume One, 23, 41–3, 48, 84n19, 85, 87, 95, 126n55, 134n87
Marx, Karl and Engels, Friedrich,
  The Holy Family, 7, 9, 120n34,
  The German Ideology, 1, 11, 23n10, 28, 30, 37, 38n9, 39, 40, 42, 46, 61, 64n9, 67, 75, 88n35, 102–3, 122, 125–8,133
Mode, 23–4, 33–4, 54, 68, 71, 76, 103, 104, 116, 124
Mode of Production, 3, 12, 66, 70, 84, 93

Nature, 5n12, 11, 16, 31n14, 32, 54–6, 58, 60, 66, 68, 77, 92–3, 102, 103, 117, 121, 124, 126, 133, 137
  History and, 36–49, 50, 52, 53, 54, 74–5
  Human beings and, 22–6, 28, 29, 54, 79, 81, 82, 84, 85, 101, 104–8, 120
Negri, Antonio, 15, 131

Ontology, 16–17, 18, 19, 24, 106, 107, 120–1, 139

Plekhanov, Georgi, 15, 16–17
Production, viii–x, 3, 5, 10, 11, 16, 29, 30, 31, 37–45, 48, 55, 58, 81, 83, 87n32, 90, 103, 107, 110, 116, 117–18, 122, 125, 126–31, 133–5
  Forces of, 63, 64, 65, 67, 97, 123, 127, 128, 130

  Relations of, 30, 38, 54, 60, 63, 64, 65, 67, 68, 117, 127, 128

Schmidt, Alfred, 54n65, 55, 56, 106n16
Second Nature, 9–10, 37
Social Relations, viii, ix, 25, 26, 28, 30, 38, 49, 53, 54, 56, 57, 62, 63, 65–8, 90, 119, 120
Species-Being, 26, 44, 46, 49, 50, 51, 53, 72, 75, 76, 104, 105
Spinoza
  Ethics, 17, 19, 23–5, 27, 28n4, 31n14, 32, 33, 58, 72, 73, 74, 76, 116, 118n28, 121
  Political Treatise, 38
  Theological-Political Treatise, 19
Subject, vii–ix, 18, 45, 46, 47, 50, 72, 77, 78, 90, 101, 104, 105, 106, 107, 117, 121, 135, 139, 140
  As Alienation, 6–8, 10, 11, 26, 69, 79–85, 87, 87n32, 94–100, 123–5
  History of, 3–5, 10, 12, 44, 52, 56, 88, 89, 115, 116, 119–20, 130, 131, 141–3
  See also Worker

Tosel, André, 15, 18
Unconscious, 73, 105, 105n14, 106, 106n15

Vaysse, Jean-Michel, 13n4, 35n24, 106n15, 113n13

Work ix–x, 6, 12, 23, 37, 40, 41, 42n22, 44, 48, 83, 84, 85, 87n32, 89, 92–5, 98, 116, 124, 132n80, 138
Worker 29, 83, 89, 90, 92–7, 122–5, 131, 133, 139–40